OVERLOAD

A BROTHER, A WAKE, AND A SECRET

OVERLOAD

a brother, a wake, and a secret

LYDIA LITTLE

SWEENEY & O'DONOVAN

ISBN: 978-1-7399949-3-8

Published by
SWEENEY & O'DONOVAN LTD.
Ballyhillow, Leap, Skibbereen, West Cork, Ireland

www.sweeneyodonovan.ie

Printed by Totem,
ul. Jacewska 89
88-100 Inowrocław
Poland

I have been faithful to my own memory of events and dialogue over the week and anniversary of my Brother's death. Others may remember things differently. I have written from the heart, and my intention is not to harm.

Saudade

A longing tinged with nostalgia, madness and sickness over something you have lost (Portuguese).

Caointeoireacht

Keening, a lament (Irish).

Discombobulated

Having self-possession upset, thrown into confusion.

Overload

To load to excess, to overburden.

Offload

Relieve oneself of a problem or worry by talking to someone else.

THE NINE CONTEMPLATIONS OF ATISHA

DEATH is inevitable. Our life span is decreasing continuously. Death will come, whether or not we are prepared for it. Human life expectancy is uncertain. There are many causes of death. The human body is fragile and vulnerable. At the time of death, our material resources are not of use to us. Our loved ones cannot keep us from death. Our own body cannot help us at the time of our DEATH.

PROLOGUE

This story starts at the end. The end of my Brother.

Dead.

For years, we had been expecting him to die, and then he went and died unexpectedly.

He didn't give us the penance of agonising over hospital machines and tubes. There was no infection or virus this time. No rantings, paranoia, or indecisions. No, this time was quick, clean and, frustratingly, a solo experience. There were no witnesses. And there was no coming back from this one.

The death certificate states it was bronchopneumonia but I know that is not the full story. In fact, there are four of us who know it was not. Four sworn to secrecy. And then it became six because someone let it slip. Then, seven, because someone decided that someone else should know. Eight, if I were to include a priest. But only under the sacrament of penance. Seal of confession and all that.

And yet, secrecy is futile now. Because after this you too will know.

But that is for the end of my story.

At first it was the ambulance crew that saw him out. My Brother called them himself. There is a debate on how long that 999 call lasted. The nurses at the hospital reported to my Mother and me: 'Sixteen minutes'.

My Brother's phone log displays something different. The call disconnected.

What was happening in between?

In any case, the ambulance crew pulled him back and, ultimately it was my Mother who was with him in the end. At least that is what she tells us. To soften the blow perhaps.

But I couldn't let it rest. Or it wouldn't rest with me. What was the true sequence of events? Those final moments before he took his last. His real last. His own last. Before the ambulance crew and their chest pumping and bag of adrenaline took over.

TUESDAY

February 2

'We don't even know his arrangements,' my Father states, as he pours himself the first of many whiskeys.

'Well, he wanted to be cremated,' my older Sister says. 'He told me that.'

Mother lights a cigarette at her window desk. Gazing out the rain spattered glass, my eye follows hers to the garden patio beyond. There is a magpie infiltrating a bird feeder that swings from the gazebo, the bird's feathers shining sapphire, emerald, and amethyst. Orca of the sky.

'I know,' I confess quietly.

My Sister frowns. Mother turns. I catch her eye.

'I wrote them down,' I say. 'Well, they're more notes than anything formal, but I did get him to sign it.' I tease a smile, trying to inject some humour. 'I told him no one would believe me otherwise.'

'What do you mean?' my Sister asks, as if offended I might know something she does not.

I drop my smile and take a controlled gentle breath, involuntarily pulling second-hand smoke into my chest, adding to a dark cloud accumulating there. It is poisonous. For the sake of peace, say nothing. I swallow the resentment and it tastes of tobacco. The heat stings. The ice clinks in my Father's glass.

'I'll get it,' I say, and shove the kitchen chair to standing. My Sister's eyes are rimmed with tears.

'You'll laugh,' I say, smiling at her reassuringly. 'Seriously.'

Turning, I leave the kitchen, but not before kissing my Father on his tear-streaked cheek.

My Brother's house is dark. Windows frame blackness fathoms deep. The gentle hill that slopes between the adjacent rural houses now acts as a Bridge of Woe. The front door is unlocked, as usual, but there is no heart here now. I consciously stop myself from calling out, 'Hey Ferg', and then, not quick enough to restrain myself, unconsciously glance to his bedroom door. Too late. I see his empty bed in there. Bare. His orthopaedic mattress deflated, his silk duvet stacked with his multitude of pillows pillar high. Vacant. I swallow. Saliva slips over the lump of loneliness in the back of my throat. Head down, I scurry into his conservatory, the hub of his house, to the filing cabinet there that metaphorically encapsulates his life. The envelope I seek is hidden between the pocket of 'Household Bills' and 'Important Documents'. I had marked it 'Website'. An impulsive disguise invented on the day.

I go there now in my mind's eye. Seven months before, July of the previous year. My Brother holding command, sipping his tepid drink through his extended straw, the large pint glass filled with muddy water that he liked to call tea. My Eldest, repairing the découpage on his latest art project – a life-size model orangutan "Mrs Freeborn and her Black Apple: A Jungle Art project – endangered species".

I was there in the capacity of his bookkeeper, filing receipts and helping clear his in-tray while he and my Eldest worked away in the background.

Strategical or planning the inevitable, I asked my Brother if now was a good time to make a note of his passwords and logins. 'Best to have them down somewhere,' I say. 'Just in case,' I add with a wink. The topic of death broached with humour, as always, on my part.

'While we're at it, do you want to talk about...,' I hesitate, '...your plans?'

My Eldest works on. I am conscious of her ear wigging and yet appreciate the witness. There is a click and brief whirr of my Brother's wheelchair as he fidgets his universe; a learned quirk whenever he is uncomfortable with something that someone has asked. Cogs of his chair mirroring the cogs of his mind as it processes.

'I'm not talking wills here,' I reassure him. 'I don't want to know those details. But like, do you want to be cremated? How do you feel about organ donation?' He is still. I pause, wondering if I have pressed somewhere too sensitive. My Eldest crosses the room and pastes a new piece of shredded National Geographic paper to the hairline of the morphing sculpture, a side glance and shy smile from her implying her coded compliance. There is the click and the whirr as he approaches me.

'Suppose now is as good as any,' he says.

I flip the page over, pen poised. Anticipating. Ready. Silence feeding the necessity of planning, and then my Brother begins. My Eldest working on his installation while he plans his removal.

It is days later when I ask my Eldest as we sit at the big dining table in my Mother's house, 'So how did ye work it?' The table is strewn with portfolio, photographs and incomplete art projects, all vying to be selected for her college portfolio. She is showing me a photo of Mrs Freeborn that was in among the mix. The great ape stares back at me with her lifelike eyes.

'First, we went through the National Geographic magazines for colour and interesting patterns. Ferg knew how he wanted her to look,' my Eldest explains. 'Gold for hair, red for her face, you know. Then we cut or shredded the pages and would use blue-tac to position the pieces. Ferg would rotate around her to get the overview. We cut out hundreds of eyes and tacked them in place. Some were kids, some babies; he rejected them all until we found the right ones. Only then would we glue them.'

My Eldest smiles as she remembered something. 'Did you know that Ferg was the only artist to contact the sculptor? You know the guy who makes the jungle art moulds?'

I shake my head.

'It is the same guy that makes all the orangutans. And all of the dozens of artists that have worked them, Ferg was the only one ever to contact him to tell him his plans for her. Find out if it was male or female.'

'Of course,' I say, smiling. 'Of course he did.'

'It's female. So that's why she became Mrs Freeborn. Otherwise she might have been Bob Freeborn or something.'

'Why Freeborn?' I ask, although I feel I have asked the obvious.

''Coz we are all born free,' my Eldest explains, rolling her eyes. 'Man, animals, we are all free the moment we are born.'

'Did you ever get to show him your picture of him as the caterpillar, you know, in your Alice in Wonderland sketch?' I ask as I look down at her range of wonderful talent.

'Oh don't even go there, Mom,' she says, offended. 'He was supposed to be helping me with my portfolio.' She is exasperated, slapping some sheets onto her A2 folder.

'I know, honey,' I say as I stroke her shoulder. 'He never got to read my new book either.' The cloud in my chest shifts a bit. 'He was going to print it out to read but....' I reach for one of her graffiti pieces.

'These are really great, Hun. Really great.'

My hand hasn't left her shoulder. It sucks at the heat and life that pulsates there.

Back in my Mother's house, I open the brown envelope and unfold the white A4 paper within. All eyes in the smoke-filled breakfast-room are on me. Eager for solace. Enlightenment even.

I review my haphazard, rushed notes. They are disorganised, crammed into the top third of the photocopy sheet of paper. Mentally, I criticise my own penmanship, the lack of professional layout. No bullet points even. Half sentences and shorthand jotted shyly. I remember feeling anxious and embarrassed to have coerced my Brother into doing it.

The first word is written boldly and underlined: '*Cremated*.'

Choosing my words, I seek my Sister's eye and say: 'You were right, he wanted to be cremated.'

She smiles with satisfaction.

'He wanted his ashes scattered. Some in De Barra's and some in, is it Namish Castle? The rest for Li.'

'Namish Castle?' my Father asks. Again I look to my Sister who I know will understand.

'Namest,' my Sister corrects. 'It's where we were for the festival in the Czech Republic.' She nods her head and tears brim again.

'He loved his time there,' she says between sniffles. 'Up till Glen's week here, it was his best time ever.' She reaches for a tissue.

My mind recalls my Brother's account of his tour abroad. All I see are his sparkling blue eyes and rosy cheeks in his telling. How he would blink rapidly when excited or happy in the reliving of a tale or a special moment. I glance back to the sheet of wishes. There is a question mark after 'organ donation'. He couldn't decide at the time. There was something 'Armchair Thriller' about donating his eyes to someone who would end up looking at the world through his. But this is irrelevant now. His unexpected death and delayed hospitalisation eliminated any possibility of organ donation.

My Sister says, 'Didn't he want a wicker casket?'

I brighten on having an accomplice. 'Yes! – It's not in my notes, but I know he didn't want a regular one.'

My Father frowns and swipes his hand over his eyes and face, exhausted already.

'Jesus, where are we supposed to get a wicker coffin?'

My Husband speaks: 'The undertakers will be able to organise all that, don't worry. They are quite common now.'

Fidgeting on my seat, I say, 'There's more.' I look around at the faces all staring at me. 'He wanted his boots sticking out of the end.'

'What?' My Father tilts his ear at me as if his hearing aids have failed him.

'His boots,' I repeat, smiling sadly, remembering my Brother's humour on the day. 'He wanted them stuck on the end of the coffin. So it would look like the coffin was too small for him.'

'Or that he was kicking out his feet, free like,' my Sister interprets. I nod. She sucks at her cigarette, satisfied.

My Father tuts and sighs next to me. On the verge of dismissing it all.

Feeling brave, I continue: 'And he wanted smiley faces stuck along the sides and an umbrella....'

'Ah we can't, Jesus...,' my Father groans.

My notes fail me and I reboot my mind trying to remember. I want to fill the gap. 'Well, he actually wanted a hand sticking out the side, holding an umbrella with Chinese writing on it. Something about a song?' I look to my Sister, hoping she knows.

She nods now, blowing out more smoke. 'Is it Ti-Ti?'

I don't know what she means.

'The song he wrote for Li?'

That clicks a switch.

'Yes, that was it.' We are both smiling now. A team. Together. Her and me. We are sisters now. Just us. No longer what was *Them*. Him and Her. But rather, her and me. We. And I feel the cloud again, and there is a space there for her. To share in it.

'Why the umbrella?' my Father asks.

'Like in his lyrics,' I stab, *'So, she's ready to fly,'* singing the tune badly, forgetting the rest of the words.

'Like Mary Poppins,' my Sister jokes. One of our childhood Christmas movies. The memories that brings up break my heart again. Tears well.

'When did he do this with you?' my Father asks, nodding towards my notes.

I check the date, the signature next to it.

'July,' I say, '29th July.'

I show him the page, reluctant to give it up. At the end of my scrawls is my Brother's signature. His written initials 'fof' and his two accompanying dots.

The 'fof' sitting there like a blister on the page.

The kitchen is flooded with smoke. It has become the hub. Our war-room. The air saturated with diplomacy, stimulants and wi-fi.

My Niece has been delegated the duty of secretary. Poised with pen and a fresh A4 page, she looks to her grandfather as he darts nouns at her, pausing in between each one.

'Coffin. Death Notice. Wake. Flowers.' With each word she glances upwards. My Husband nods and mouths: 'Undertakers.'

She understands she must write whatever her grandfather dictates. The rest of us all know that it will be all co-ordinated by the funeral home but allow my Father to carry on. This is what he needs to do.

My Husband finds what he has been looking for on his iPhone and, dialling a number, leaves the room. On return he waits for a gap and lets my Father know that the O'Sullivan undertakers will be here in the morning at 9.30.

'I thought we would use the local ones?' my Father asks, flummoxed.

'They are,' my Husband explains gently. 'They took over Arundel's a while ago. They run a lot of the West Cork funeral homes now.'

My Father nods and sighs again.

'Li won't get in till late Wednesday night.' He is referring to my Sister-in-Law. My Brother's Chinese wife. 'We can't decide anything till then.'

It is only Tuesday. My Brother is only hours dead. I glance over to my niece. She is shading in the corner of the A4 page. Rapid lines of blackness brim over the edge, gravitational forces and matter trapped within. The pen traces back and forth over the same lines again and again and again.

My cloud pulses in my chest as I imagine my Sister-in-Law and her son flying in a similar darkness from Japan. Flying the jet stream. Her own inner blackness engulfing her.

She had only just set down and had to turn around to come home again.

'Thank God Deng is with her,' I say.

My Father had to plan the breaking of the news to my Brother's wife. Time it right. Anticipating when my Brother's wife would land in Japan. Waiting to call his Step-grandson. So they could console each other. The dread of it. Extinguishing the excitement of their reunion. Terminating her pilgrimage to China (via Japan to collect her son) where they should celebrate Chinese New Year, their Spring Festival. The moving feast, like our Easter, shifts with the new moon. Spring Festival would never mean the same again.

That Skype call had been difficult. Death is never welcome in any language.

'They will fly back into Dublin around 9pm,' my Father says. 'She will be exhausted. Someone will have to meet her.'

My Father has the look we know too well. He means himself.

'You can't go,' my Sister states. 'You need to be here.'

I see a flicker of something in my Father's eye. The need, or is it a want, to escape? Perhaps it is one merging into the other.

'There'll be loads coming down,' I offer as an alternative. 'James, Marc, Mal.' I realise that the list of my Brother's Dublin friends could be endless. 'One of them will meet her.'

'She'll need to rest before she comes down,' my Father says.

'She'll want to come straight down, knowing Li,' my Sister declares with confidence. "I wouldn't put it past her to jump in a taxi direct to West Cork. She wouldn't care what it would cost.'

'I'd better ring the lads,' my Father says and strays from the room.

I follow the line of the hall from the kitchen down the corridor to my Father's study. The door is ajar, and I can see he is on the phone. It is a familiar scene but in this one his face is different. It is not the look of efficiency or energy that he has for business; nor is it the gentle eye and smiling face natural for friends or social calls. It is a new look. Ashen. Lined. Furrowed. Frowned. I don't like this new skin. It is of an old man. Not that of my Father.

Hearing his broken English, I know he is talking to my Sister-in-Law. She is on speaker-phone. In the twenty-two years she has lived here, her English still hovers around nouns sung like notes in staccato. Like a Morse code of dashes and dots that we often struggle to cipher.

'Heart?' She asks. I presume she wants to know what got my Brother in the end. Something to mull over on the return leg of her journey.

'We-are-not-sure-Li,' my Father says, enunciating each word tonelessly. Slowly. 'He-stopped-breathing.' And then more naturally, 'Maybe his lung stop working.'

My Father moves from his office chair to his couch. He is already exhausted. I sit at the other end. To both give and seek comfort. My cloud shifts in my chest, anxious, tugging at my rib cage.

'Infection?' she asks and then we hear her relay some Chinese to someone at her end.

'No Li, no infection.' My Father pinches the bridge between his eyes. 'It was quick, Li. No pain.'

'He alone?' she asks.

I feel a stab and look to my Father.

'Maureen was with him at the end,' he says. It is not a lie.

Despite modern technology, the call echoes and sounds smothered.

'Who?'

'Mama-Maureen.' My Father explains, a little louder.

'Ahh, Mama with him. Good, good,' she says with satisfaction. 'Maureen there now?'

My Father shakes his head and then says, 'Lydia is here.'

At that moment my Sister appears at the door way and walks in.

'And Shar.'

I shout, 'Hi Li.' My Sister echoes me.

Li says something I do not catch and my Father sits forward as if to hear her better. Something about a car and crash. I look to my Father. He looks as confused as I.

I whisper, 'Is she asking about Colin?'

Our Musician Friend had died Tuesday of last week following a coma as a result of a car crash. My Brother was due to sing at the funeral service tomorrow, Wednesday.

'She knows he is dead already,' my Sister say s impatiently, dismissing my theory. My Sister grumbles something else that I do not catch. I ignore it. Then I remember another West Cork friend whose car had more recently skidded on black ice. Poxed with luck, that friend ricocheted back into life after that near miss. Maybe that is who my

Sister-in-Law is talking about. There had been no update on our lucky friend's recovery when my Sister-in-Law left the country forty-eight hours before. Perhaps she is asking about her.

Leaning towards the phone I call out: 'Do you mean Helen, Li? She is fine.' And then add shouting a bit louder, 'She is alive.'

My Sister says something else that I do not catch and then we are interrupted by a shriek down the phone.

'Liar? Why Sharon call me liar?'

I am thrown by the sudden outburst.

'What?' My Sister winces, aghast.

My Father and I both talk at the same time, adding to the confusion. My Sister-in-Law is shouting in Chinese now on the other side.

'Oh for God's sake,' my Sister exclaims. She slumps into an armchair near the door.

'Where did that come from?' I mouth.

My brain frantically processes the last bits of conversation. Replaying what I had said. And then it clicks.

'No, Li. Helen, Helen is ALIVE. No one is saying you are a liar. We said, Helen is A-Live,' I explain, desperately emphasising the 'alive'.

'Jesus,' my Father grimaces and takes the phone off speaker phone.

'Li, Vince here.' He watches as my Sister leaves the room, rolling her eyes.

'We will get someone to meet you at the airport. You arrive Dublin nine-thirty, night time, yes?'

I stretch out my hand offering to take the phone. He hands it over, eagerly.

'Li, it's Lydia.'

Her greeting is a melodic: 'Oh ahh' combination, almost singing my name. She is sweet once more.

'Li, we will get someone to meet you at the airport,' I explain.

And in that moment I remember the time my Father and Sister went to China to visit my Sister-in-Law's family. Because my Brother was unable to go (not a good place for him and his disability), his sister and the family patriarch went in his stead. My Sister acted as chaperone. It would not have been proper for my Father to travel alone with his daughter-in-law who travelled without her husband. My Sister, by accompanying them, fixed all that.

The entire clan greeted them at the airport. With flowers and bowing and the Chinese welcome of fist-against-palm salute. It was a great honour, marking both their arrival and the significance of their journeying to China.

It is important that we have someone there to meet my Sister-in-Law off the plane now too. Three possible friends come to mind. My Brother's boarding school Poet Friend I would have to exclude, as he was coming from a different direction. And so I am left with two. I hadn't even spoken to them yet but trusted their friendship and loyalty to my Brother and our family not to let us down.

With this in mind, I empower her by asking, 'Who would you like to collect you?' I offer: 'James or Marc?'

'James,' she declares. My Brother's other boarding schoolfriend and Original Band Member. I look to my Father and he nods satisfactorily. Without another word, I hand the phone back to my Father who wraps up the call with a promise to have the Original Band Member meet them and a command to make sure she gets some sleep on the plane.

All is good again, for now.

I am taking a break from the smoke-filled war room and stand at the hall door. Sucking in the clean cool night air. The sky is mottled with stars and slush-like cloud. I wonder where my Brother is now. Are his molecules up there somewhere, looking down on us all? I glance down towards my Brother's house, looking beyond the music studio that sits half way on the Bridge of Woe, to the new abyss beyond. The studio spotlight flashes on, and my Husband's silhouette is a-glow, walking towards me now.

'What is that for?' I ask crossly, looking at the camera that is in his hands.

'I took photos,' he states innocently.

I am offended. What or why could he have good reason to be taking photographs? The world is miserable with misery. How could he not know that? There is nothing to celebrate. To mark. No moment to snap.

'I thought it should be captured,' he says gently.

'What?' I ask, my temper short.

'As he left it.'

My cloud swells. And then retracts swiftly within me. Like a retreating wave. Loosens its grip on my ribs. I understand. He need not explain.

'Before things get moved about. Shifted like.'

My inner eye sees my Brother's bedroom with his bed and hoist and trays opposite his TV, Sky box and video player. Bedside trolley stacked with tablets and TV controls, feeding bowls and pint glasses. The room cluttered with towels and discarded socks. Out of the way, neatly positioned, sit his boots and wheel chair. In the corner, disregarded boxes of adult nappies. Bed post disguised by his hanging cardigans, hat and scarf. His wife's half bed tucked in beside his. Duvet rolled back on itself. Flip-flops, Chinese slippers and shoe boxes shoved underneath. Her bedside locker strewn with wet wipes, hand sanitiser, hand lotion and Chinese kitsch. In his conservatory, dining tables heavily laden with brushes, canvasses, paints, and pens. Work in progress, rejected works, paint testers. His torn-up magazines and notebooks and overflowing in-tray. On another surface, his computer and studio equipment, microphones, speakers. In the corner, his piano. Washing lines hang from the curtain poles, sagging with drying art work.

All would be shifted to make room for the Wake. Never to be the same again. Whisked away. Wiped. And my wonderful, dear, insightful Husband had the intuition to capture it all before my Brother's world would be gone.

My Husband's photos. A record. A snap shot of my Brother's life. To be archived.

As it was.

As it should be.

Forever more.

Amen.

CLOUD

1) A visible mass of condensed watery vapour floating in the atmosphere, typically high above the general level of the ground. 2) Used to refer to a state or cause of gloom, suspicion, trouble, or worry

CLOUD TYPES

LOW CLOUDS

Cumulus – detached, generally dense clouds with sharp outlines

Stratus –grey cloud, produces drizzle, ice prisms or snow grains.

Stratocumulus – honeycomb

Cumulonimbus – thunderstorm cloud, heavy and dense

MID CLOUDS

Altostratus - grey or bluish cloud sheets or layers

Altocumulus – white or grey patch, sheet or layered 'cotton balls'

Nimbostratus – continuous rain cloud

HIGH CLOUDS

Cirrus – white delicate filaments 'mare's tails'

Cirrostratus – milky veil of fog

Cirrocumulus – 'mackerel sky'

Molecular Cloud (aka Stellar nursery) – accumulation of interstellar gas & dust

'God Cloud' – isolated, towering vertical cloud

Cocoon
Wisps
Airmass
Skud
Blanket
Heaps
Fusion
Smother
Puff
Haze
Vapour
Suspended
Veil
Smog
Gloom
Fog
Cloud
Mist
Droplets
Altostratus
mass
Stratus
atmosphere
high
downwards
Sliver
slumped
watery
chest
suspicion
light
God
Cumulonimbus
GodCloud
trouble
Condensed
Floating
Cirrus
Rain
Cumulus
Visible
golden
worry
swelling
Stratocumulus
Cirrocumulus

IT BEGINS.

I have just spun through work's revolving doors to head home when I get an emotional, almost unintelligible, call from my Father.

'Whereareyounow?'

'I'm in Cork, just came away from our quarterly meeting.'

Already I know it is my Brother. A rotary of possibilities dials up in my head.

'It's Ferg. He's not breath…,' he couldn't finish the word for tears. 'I think this is it.'

'I'm on my way,' I gasp, hanging up.

Discombobulated, I scurry in half circles trying to remember where I parked my car and, on finding it, struggle with keys and kit and exiting. My head pushes through some logic and I realise the ambulance must be coming to Cork, so a panicked drive home to West Cork would be futile. I can't ring my Father. Or rather, won't. I need practicality. Stability. No emotion. I call my Mother instead.

'Mom, it's me. What's the story with Ferg?'

'Who rang you?' she asks suspiciously.

'Dad.'

'Oh, okay.' She takes a breath. She explains that the Home Help had found him. 'He wasn't breathing.'

'Oh my God. Is he okay?'

And then think, if she is on the phone to me now, who is with him?

'Is there someone with him now?'

'The ambulance crew are with him. Doctor Finlay is here too.'

The panic in me recedes.

'Oh, okay. Good. Good.'

I realise my own breath is caught somewhere in the back of my throat. I take a deep breath, sucking in cool light air into my belly.

'Where are they bringing him, to Cork or Bantry?' I ask, knowing my Brother's favourite was Bantry.

'I don't know yet, I'll call you back.'

I accept this and hang up. American like. With no 'Bye' or 'Talk to you in a bit.'

I trawl through Cork Airport Industrial Estate in my car, mindless, cruising from one parking zone to the next, not wanting to leave the security of my work environment. I decide to park. I try to call my Sister, then my Niece, who also works up here in the Estate. My Husband is the only one to pick up. Instinctively he knows something is wrong. I am making gurgling noises down the phone.

'Breathe,' he commands. 'Breathe.'

So it is Bantry, and I make my way west. Recalling nothing of my journey, muscle memory driving the car except for one clear precise time grab. A clarity within. Where I realise that Bantry is *not* good. My mind replays the original phone call with my Father and his raw emotion. This is not a reoccurrence of a twisted bowel or trapped gas.

I am on the Dunmanway road heading west, driving through the low valley of Murragh, and my mind grips that specific moment, a geometric slice in time where everything is suspended and there is a celestial shift.

Bantry is a stay. Bantry is a stopping place.

The rain ceases, and a sliver of golden light reaches downward towards the earth from a divine cumulus – a God cloud. Bursting from the airwaves flows a haunting crescendo of *pedal steel* strings and clouded lyrics of a song I have never heard before.

I don't want to wait anymore.
I'm tired looking for answers.
Take me to some place where there is music and laughter.
I don't know if I'm scared of dying but I'm scared of living;
Too fast, too slow, regret, remorse;
Hold on; no, I gotta go.

And in that instant I know he is gone. My Brother is dead.

I hear a voice calling, calling out for me.
These shackles I've made in an attempt to be free.
Be it for reason, be it for love.
I won't take the easy road. Easy road. The easy road.
Show me my silver lining, I try to keep on keeping on.
Show me my silver lining, I try to keep on keeping on.

Parking at Bantry hospital, I turn off the engine and allow its energy to dissipate. I take stock. If what I feel is true, then I must register this moment. My life is about to change. I wait for the last hum and ticking of the car's innards to ease, and mine with them. Disentangling from my motor cocoon, I take another breath and snatch a last view of the world as I know it. I take my phone and tissues, my purse, abandoning my bulky handbag to the car.

I am stopped adjacent to the hospital ambulance parking bay and I see West Cork's two serving vehicles resting there for now. It is not often the two are docked at the same time, and I realise that one of them has just brought my Brother here.

Movement by the building's side door catches my eye and I recognise the crewman smoking a cigarette. He is a familiar face from a previous life and would pass me sometimes on the road in his new official capacity as a paramedic. I had seen him once or twice over the years at my Brother's house. The 999 call-outs had become almost social.

Our eyes lock and I feel a lump come unstuck at the back of my throat. I want to ask but can't, because the truth might hurt and I'm not ready for it yet.

'Brendan.' I say, acknowledging him. He nods at me.

'I won't ask,' I blurt and scurry by.

'Don't,' I hear him say to the back of me.

Sucking in a breath, I make my way in through the hospital back doors. Familiarity brings me along the corridor, past the lifts, up the steps, bypassing the main entrance and reception. I avoid all eye contact. Instinct brings me to intensive care, where I am guessing my Brother will be and no doubt my Mother beside him. My boots clack on the cold tiles and, rounding the corridor bend, I see the backs of both my Parents ahead of me.

Perhaps it was the familiar sound of my gait or telepathy, but they both turn as if dancing a slow duet, and I lock eyes with my Mother. She shakes her head, pulling her mouth downwards and steps forward towards me. Arms outstretched.

I may not be ready for the news yet. But it is ready for me.

Relinquishing, I take it in – as if a heap of grey stratocumulus has come in from the sea, infiltrating my chest, fusing to my ribs. Like an unearthly downpour that comes in sheets, knocking me horizontal.

There is nothing like a warm, loving embrace. My Father dishes them out readily and in turn will receive them gratefully. My Mother does not. The family joke is how my Father is like a chocolate Malteser with a ball bearing core, my Mother, the ball bearing with a Malteser core. A hug from my Mother usually is requested by us in advance and even then it is limp armed, or a token pat-pat, with a flat cheek offered, whereupon we are permitted to place a kiss. I do not doubt my Mother's love for me, for us. It is a tough love. Sometimes a cruel-to-be-kind love. It is what has helped her survive her own life cycle. And has helped us survive ours.

So, in that moment when my Mother's arms are outstretched, I accept them willingly and abandon my Father briefly while he looks on. My Mother wraps her arms around me and takes the weight of me onto her chest, braces herself for the full impact of my sobbing head into her shoulder. It is her gift to me of unadulterated tenderness and solace.

Squeezing my eyes shut, breathing in her warmth and Opium scent, I shut out the world beyond and escape into the dark comfort that holds me now. It whispers to me and I realise it is my Mother's voice: 'It is for the best. He went the way he wanted to.'

I draw back from her heat, nodding, reaching for my tissues.

'Do you know, I have to say I am delighted for him?' she continues as if he has just been awarded a Grammy.

I blow my nose and, bewildered, look over to my Father. He is stood there, red-eyed and shook looking. I step into him now and give him a familiar full-bear hug. This time I am not sure who is comforting who. That done, we automatically start down the corridor and my Mother continues from where she left off.

'While I know we will miss him, he really is better off.'

'What happened?' I manage.

And that is when my Mother tells me the first version of how she found my Brother dead.

I follow my Parents into the intensive care ward where my Brother remains behind a flimsy curtain. Separating him from the living. This side of the curtain there are others who struggle to breathe and live and recover, and there he is, on the other side, having left us. Gone somewhere else.

It is as if I am in the wings and it is that tense moment before the lights dim and the stage curtains are pulled back. My stomach clenches and my breath catches in the back of my throat.

I slip into the small enclosed hospital space.

Hospital beds are a familiar sight with their gadgets, monitors, tubes, and intervention. There is none of that now. There is an intense silence and my Brother is oh so still. He looks as if he is sleeping, only I know this not to be the case. The lack of his breathing mask and portable oxygen tells me so. He is no longer *wired for sound.*

Someone has lain him on clean white bed linen, tucked him in snugly. I note the blue polka-dot hospital gown and bed spread with an oddly satisfying matching blue Celtic spiral. The cover is folded back on his chest and his arms extend over the fold as if holding it in place. Two lumps show where his knees cannot straighten and give a very relaxed look about him. His lips are tinged an unsettling blue grey, slightly separated, as if mid-snore. His cheeks, pale and relaxed looking. Unshaven, his enthusiasm to grow a full gringo moustache is still evident but for the slightly mocking lack of definition or recent grooming.

I observe all this in the moment it takes to be at his side.

Leaning in to place my forehead against his, I am surprised at the warmth of him still. Kissing his tepid cheek, I reach for his hand. Cup my fingers into his. It is a familiar hold. I had never noted it till now. But it is our hold. His fingers are cooler. As if he had just come in from the cold.

Instinctively, I rub them to bring some life back into him.

In an unspoken agreement we take turns in staying with my Brother. As if to keep watch in case he is not dead after all. My Father is focused on my Brother's iPhone, using his contacts to reach out and break the news. I too look at my phone and think up a list of who I need to call. Not who needs me calling them but with whom I need to speak myself. My Sister is already on the way, so that obligation is covered. I must ring my Husband and leave my Brother's space to do so. And then I think of my daughters. They are back in boarding school only twenty-four hours after the Wake of our Music Friend and will have to endure heartache all over again. Quickly realising that classes would soon be over and their mobile phones redistributed, I feared what thread and status might be posted on Facebook for them to learn the news second-hand. I need to reach them before the virtual world snares them in the grip of comments and emoticons. But to call them now would mean no one is beside them when I break the news. School protocol dictates that I call the school in advance so they can have the school nurse or counsellor primed and ready. But wouldn't it be best to have a member of the family there to deliver the news in person? My mind is deferring a decision. I can't make any independently.

Stalling a moment in the hospital corridor. I recognise one of the male orderlies approaching, pushing an empty wheelchair. It is the same man who attended my Brother the last time we were here. Who pushed him from the ward to the x-ray department. My Brother still alive, laid uncomfortably on the sterile gurney, in severe pain but still sharing jokes while I trotted along beside him holding his pillows in place. Here is the same man now, and I wonder does he recognise me. He passes me and offers a gentle smile. I realise that all staff do this. It is the smile of acknowledgement that covers the necessary etiquette without offending. After all, any lay person in the corridor might be the bearer of any and every emotion. The hospital smile is a safe one. Any sincere smile could be perceived as insensitive. Gauche. I give the safe smile back in turn. All the while inside I am screaming *'Do you not know my Brother is dead? How can you smile at me so? My beautiful big Brother is dead.'*

My Husband picks up after a few rings.

'Hey.' His voice is gentle, soft, quiet. It is his 'I am at work' voice.

'He's gone,' I manage.

'No,' he says. There is a gap. 'Are you serious?'

As if I would joke about something like that and he knows it. His question is Tourette's like. I have already forgiven him.

'The girls,' I say and can't finish the sentence for crying.

'I'm on the way,' he says.

'Okay,' I reply and hang up. Again, American like. And realise I don't know if he means on the way to me here in Bantry or to Dingle to get the girls.

Following a few calls to close friends, avoiding details as much as possible, I return to the intensive care room and pass an older couple who are hanging back at the nurse's station. The old man they are keeping vigil over struggles for breath on the far side of the ward beyond my Brother. The woman glances over to the old man and back to me again. Our eyes meet and the unspoken is exchanged.

'Mine is dead. Yours will follow.'

'Yours is dead. Mine will follow.'

We both exchange the safe smile.

Behind my Brother's curtain my Father sits alone, leaning forward over my Brother's phone.

'Have you rung Marc?' I ask quietly as I sit next to him. He would be first on my list of Brother's friends to be called. Having met my Brother as a fan back in the mid-eighties – attending gigs, helping with posters, merchandising, taking photos – he soon formed a close friendship with my Brother and band, even drumming for them once or twice, and over time became the unofficial band archivist.

My Father nods: 'He's calling the gang.'

I understand. This means my Brother's band, his Dublin friends; anyone of importance on the band mailing list would get a personal call from The Archivist who is as close to a second Brother as I could get.

'Aileen?'

'She's stuck in Mexico, trying to get out.'

By profession she is now an art curator, a private buyer for one of the world's respected art galleries. She met my Brother when she was a student American tourist back in the eighties. And never left Europe. Her role has varied over the years but never her loyalty to my Brother. Rumour has it they even dated briefly, but I am not so sure. Based now in the UK, her latest project involves traveling the world to seek new talent. I imagine a hermit painter, the next Diego Rivera, high on a hill-top cabin outside of Mexico and she frantically trying to work out the logistics of getting out.

Sitting next to my Father, I rub his knee. No words are exchanged. As much for my own comfort as his.

'Where's your mother?' he asks without looking up.

'She passed me earlier when I was on the phone,' I say, still looking at my Brother. 'Said something about going for a stroll. She had her coffee flask and book with her.'

My Mother, a smoker for more than fifty years, never goes anywhere without her fags and rarely without a flask full of coffee and a book. Even to my Brother's deathbed it would appear.

I smile at my Brother. He would have loved that.

Standing up, my Father is still texting and makes his way out.

'Are you using Ferg's phone to text people?'

'Yeah,' he says, pausing to look at me.

'Jesus, Dad, it will look as if Ferg is texting them about himself.'

'I don't have his contacts,' he grumbles. 'Anyway, I'm putting my name in them so they know it's from me,' he adds defensively.

I laugh and shake my head mockingly. My Brother would love that. As if he was already talking from the Beyond. But now is not the time to joke.

My Father leaves the curtained cocoon, and I am alone with my dead Brother. Reaching for his hand again, I register he is colder now. A patchwork of red blotches have appeared along the underside of his skin. The only two flesh parts visual are his head and neck and his arms. Everything else is tucked into the hospital garb. I am no doctor but I understand gravity enough to know that the decomposition process is in the early stages. His blood pooling within him. His blood congealing, settling within.

THE NINE CEMETERY CONTEMPLATIONS OF BUDDHIST MONKS

CHOSO

Distension

KAISO

Rupture

KETSUZUSO

Exudation of blood

NORANSO

Putrefaction

SELOSO

Discolouration and desiccation

LANSO

Consumption by animals and birds

SANSO

Dismemberment

KOSSO

Bones

SHOSO

Parched to dust

He looks good, my dead Brother. And there is a feeling of being at peace about him. It has been too long since I witnessed him not having to struggle. Even when at home, he fidgeted to get comfortable. When in bed, his automatic orthopaedic mattress adjusted itself for him. That, or his Wife. When in hospital, we would constantly have to adjust pillows under his knees, under his ankles, shift his shoulder some, move the pillow under his head. The nurses were unable to keep up with his needs. So we would dance around the bed, pushing something here, sliding something there, adjusting and settling. It was emotionally and physically exhausting. We would take turns to stay with him. His Wife naturally was his number one, and my Sister would take over when she became too exhausted and needed a break. My Mother would replace my Sister, and I her. My Father would be on call. But we all knew, including my Brother, that my Father found such caring difficult. My Brother's Wife, my Sister and my Mother would rarely quit the rota. My Father and I returned to our own lives, picking up the pieces: helping with any neglected paperwork, business, bills or administration that needed attending during or after my Brother's hospital stay.

The many times my Brother was at Bantry he always had to remind the nursing staff that his disability meant that although he was unable to move any of his major muscle groups voluntarily, it did not mean he was paralysed. As a result, he would feel everything. Every cramp, every gut twinge, every bowel twist and stomach distention, every congested lung, every strangled breath, every pin and needle, stomach contraction, surging reflux or lung struggle, every tickle, annoying nose drip, head itch, every dry throat, urge to pee, to fart, to take a dump, every irritating nasal hair, frog-in-the-throat, every pin prick, needle and tube gagging.

He would feel all of this and not be able to do a damn thing about it. Not one damn thing.

My Brother is still now.

There are no pillows. No adjustments needed. I feel useless. Sitting there. Just me and my Brother. And then I think of my Sister-in-Law, his Wife, and wonder where in the air she is now. It must be killing her not to be here. And I think of another of my Brother's friends who has followed and recorded my Brother for the past ten years, a documentary in the making. And the two of them not here to share or capture a pivotal point in my Brother's life. I take out my own iPhone and, feeling convent-girl-like, check around me, listening to beyond the curtains. Hearing nothing, I take some photos of my Brother. Lying there dead. In the bed. Lying there dead in the bed and me taking photos of him looking all peaceful and, well, dead. And I imagine him somewhere else cracking up laughing at the nervous state of me for fear of being caught.

We are not long back from the hospital when the first of the house callers come by.

It is meant well. Or perhaps it is just tradition, but I feel it is too soon.

We are only half. My Sister's Husband, my Husband and our joint children have yet to arrive to the homestead. We haven't circled the wagons fully yet.And outsiders are already upon us.

My Father pours glasses of whiskey, and my Mother is stabbing them with her eyes.

I feel allergic to their words of condolences and sympathy, my mind playing games on me. What are no doubt kind gestures I see as exaggerated smacking of lips and eyes hungry for information. I resent their presence.

My Mother flaps about them, moving pots and pans and opening the oven door, pretending to get the dinner on. Her eyes dart to me, and I see the anger brooding there.

My Father nips out to the back kitchen and the big freezer to get ice, and I use the opportunity to let them know that the rest of the family have yet to arrive.

'If you don't mind, we need to get the dinner on and...,' I glance to the door, hoping my Father is out of earshot, '...I feel awful but I need to ask ye to go.'

My Mother appears beside me and in great Abbey Theatre style announces, 'The rest of the family have yet to arrive.' She brushes an invisible crumb from the counter-top. 'We appreciate you calling but....' She leaves the sentence hang there in its own noose.

'Of course,' they say, and with one slug, then a second, the whiskey is gone.

In true host style, my Father arrives with the ice in hand and, spying their empty glasses, is offering another. The husband is keen and about to accept but, by the grace of his wife and the daggers thrown at him by my Mother, he reconsiders and, offering an excuse and repeated condolences, they depart.

'Can you believe them?' my Mother says, and the door not quite closed on them.

'They are just paying their respects, Mom,' I say, as much to convince myself.

I am at the ready for the next callers who arrive minutes after, their car lights giving their arrival away. Word is out. My Mother and I stand sentry-like at the open front door. The callers inch forward, one foot placed over the threshold, another unzipping her jacket. As if settling in for a long one.

I need to nip this one in the bud. Trying to suppress my own negative thoughts of anticipated stalkers of the dead and those who can barely contain themselves for the want of a full Rosary or a good Wake.

Taking one of their hands, I shake it solemnly.

'Thank you so much for calling. It means a lot to us.'

'Yes,' my Mother says, standing firm next to me. Another foot is inched forward. The tightening personal space is uncomfortably narrow.

'I hope you don't mind,' I say, taking up the new family script, 'but the rest of the family have yet to arrive. We won't ask you to stay.'

There is a flicker of an eye, and the foot is taken back. A pause and the zipper is reached for again.

'Oh yes, of course,' one says. The other purses her lips and nods.

They leave, and no sooner is the door closed than I run to my Father's office, steal a blank sheet of paper from his printer and rummage in his desk for a marker. Bringing it into my Mother I start to write off the cuff.

'Can I have your Sellotape please mom?'

'The Sellotape?'

'Yes, I'm going to put a notice on the door.'

My Mother looks over my shoulder at what I am writing.

'Clever girl,' she says and, sitting at her desk, lights up a cigarette, blowing calmness back into the room.

We appreciate you calling at this sad time but the family would appreciate some private time. Thank you for your understanding.

It is seventy-two hours later when I remove the sign. Re-reading what I have written, the writer in me cringes at my repetition and poor word choice.

WEDNESDAY

February 3

My nine-year-old Son is oblivious to the change hurled at us. Last moments of innocence have been protected in the form of a last-minute sleep over. On a school night. "Best night ever."

My Husband and I had a notion that he could attend school and that his joyful bubble would remain intact. But the schoolyard can be a tactless place, and I realised he needed, I needed, the news to come from us.

'What time did you say the undertakers are coming?'

'Nine thirty,' my Husband reminds me.

It is now an hour earlier, time enough to collect our boy before school and return to Schull. We travel together to his friend's house.

He is surprised to see the two of us and at such an early hour. His enthusiasm gushing on seeing his father accompanying me on a workday.

'I'm working from home today,' my Husband lies.

Jumping into the back seat, my Son questions why I am getting in next to him. He leans back to look at me. Take it all in.

I delay in delivering my rehearsed lines and put my arm around him.

'What's wrong, Mom?' Instinct is an amazing thing. 'What is it now?' he asks hesitatingly.

The year to date has been a difficult one. And we are only in February, just. Our much-loved elderly pet dog, Ellie, had died some weeks before. My Son saw death for the first time. Then my Brother's Music Friend died last week following the car accident. My Son saw death for the second time. My boy has met death too soon in his short life.

'It's Uncle Ferg,' I manage. The cloud swelling in my chest, the lump in my throat corking my tears.

'Is he dead too?'

I croak and try to catch the lump, wanting to remain strong for my boy. Sadness bubbles up and I can only nod at him. I squeeze his shoulder towards me.

'Oh no,' he says and then leaning in, hugs me. 'You okay, Mom?'

His gentleness hits hard and tears overflow.

'What happened?' he asks, squeezing me. I am unable to answer him.

'Shortness of breath,' my Husband explains.

I manage a smile at the old family explanation why anyone has died.

My Husband starts up the car and takes us westwards.

My Son is silent a moment and then, after some pondering, turns his head up to me, 'D'ya know what is great, Mom?' His voice is perky, as if about to impart some wonderful news.

'Ferg gets to sing with Colin again. AND David Bowie. And Michael Jackson, and even Elvis. They can all jam together now.'

My heart breaks again.

'And Mom, there is no gravity where he is gone so he can walk now and dance again too.'

Sniffling back my tears, I laugh a little and jump on board his happy caravan.

'That IS a lovely idea. And do you know I imagine he will be able to play all his instruments again too. His tin whistle, his guitar, the piano…'. I dwell upon the range of talent my Brother had.

'The mouth organ, Jew's harp, trumpet…,' my Husband adds. I find his eyes locked on mine in the rear-view mirror and smile sweetly at him.

'Wow,' my Son says, 'they will have one super party.'

'They will for sure,' I say, squeezing him into me again, absorbing the joy exuding from his essence.

Feeding off it.

The family are sat at the big dining table. All eyes are on the undertaker.

He is a Pillar of neatness and pressed cleanliness and good manners. His tone is calm and eloquent with a soft brogue that reassures and settles. One with us. The unwanted friend. He of all knowledge who we hope will enlighten and sponge away our cumulonimbus.

My Father calls to order, officiates and as quickly delegates to the Pillar, who with a gentle familiarity walks us through the steps.

There is the signing over of all that remains of my Brother from the hospital to the undertakers, and we consent to a schedule for my Brother's coming home for his final send-off. Thursday is decided to be just for family, to allow time for his Wife and Stepson to return to West Cork. Friday for the Wake. And Saturday, the celebration of his life. There is to be no religious ceremony, no Rosary, no prayers at his side. My Brother could not abide structured religion. Deeply moral, with great integrity and a fascination with speculation on extra-solar planetary systems, he was a celestial magnet all on his own. The need, however, to have a venue large enough to hold his disciples and all others who loved him decreed the use of the Catholic Church. This meant we would have to meet the relevant authority halfway. We would need to negotiate around the minimum required by the Church funeral service.

There is the wording of the death notice, and we craft a paragraph that satisfies all the literary and creative around the table. Flowers? No. Donations instead to charities. The first would be the one my Brother had subscribed monthly to for many years: Sightsavers. I feel for them and the many who will now go without because of his soon-to-be cancelled direct debit. The second, our choice. While my Brother never acknowledged them formally, never financially supported them, never sponsored, nor promoted them, they were inevitably part of his life. His world. It felt right to include them now. Muscular Dystrophy Ireland.

And then there were the micro-details. The coffin. A catalogue is passed around the table. I flick through the glossy pages and marvel at the selection. It is a brochure of *boxes*, a fashion of final statements. Choices range from the trendy wicker or traditional pine to Victorian mahogany with brassy bling. There is even the out-there alternatives: superhero decals for any DC fans. O'Sullivan's has something for us all.

My Father selects the wicker, as my Brother had requested – at a high cost at which my Father doesn't even bat an eye.

And the cremation. In what would his ashes finally sit? My Sister and I inspect the range as if picking out a new ornament and inexplicably select the same. A black and silver dewdrop shaped container, small like a salt seller, equipped with plastic bottom stopper as if for the same purpose.

It is explained that as my Brother's Wife will presumably take his ashes to China, a specific type of urn will be required, as demanded by air regulations. A cardboard box. In the end my Brother's remains would be split to allow for his Wife's container, plus a few more besides. Cardboard for his air miles to China and the Czech Republic, and porcelain twins for my Sister and me. We would later select two separate urns for his Stepson and Wife.

Finally, timing.

It is decided that the Wake for friends and family will be from three on Friday. Like the Christ. My Father shares with us that the neighbours have offered to accommodate and manage car parking in their adjacent field across from us. Many are expected, and they are happy to police as necessary on the day.

Saturday's timing must fit in with the Parish Priest's commitments to his West Cork flock. There is a christening to be had on the same day.

I can't help but think, 'Out with the old, in with the new'.

'Li wants Ferg waked down at theirs,' my Father announces.

Of course, this makes sense. Even though all the while we had been talking as if my Brother would be waked at my Parents' house.

'Your Mother would be happier, anyway,' my Father adds. 'That way she won't have to deal with all the crowds.'

My Mother is not sitting with us now, preferring to leave all decisions to someone else. She will comment after the fact.

Short of signing some papers, it would appear all is done with the Pillar and we prepare to let him go.

We have twenty-four hours or so before my Brother will be returned to us. And only a few until it is our Music Friend's funeral in the village. I am not able for it.

To think my Brother was due to sing at his good friend's service. The village would turn out in all its glory to see one musician off and then have to turn around and do it all again on Saturday. Seven days between the two artist friends dying.

I threw in the jab, 'Trust Ferg to go and steal the wind from Colin's thunder.'

I only said it the once. It didn't raise the reaction I was hoping for.

Somewhere in there I managed to joke of how the first must have been there toe-tapping impatiently on the other side as if to say: 'Come on bro, don't leave me "here, on my own (again)."' Hah, bloody hah.

Nobody got it.

My Brother would have.

Following the meeting with the Pillar, my Husband understands that the planning of my Brother's celebration in the church will need to involve the approval and participation of the Parish Priest. Raised by devout Catholics, my Husband has a good understanding that the Church will have, let's say, certain demands. My Brother most certainly did not want a religious ceremony; he was not a practising Catholic, but he was spiritual and a good person.

We need to use the Church to meet our anticipated crowds and so, being respectful to both my Brother and the parish, a fine balance would have to be met.

My Husband cleverly decides to reach out to a friend for advice before meeting the Parish Priest. The friend is a former Catholic monk who converted to the Church of England and has a good understanding of what might be needed from a Catholic perspective without being overly sensitive to us not following the rules. He is also someone who provides a fair and balanced view on the Church and its ways. My Husband suggests the Reverend Friend would have a good knowledge of what was the minimum necessity on our part, and with that knowledge to hand, my Husband could then talk to the Parish Priest.

Following a phone call, the Reverend Friend arrives as promised, and soon we are sitting at the big table to hear about the format of a funeral service and what parts of a Church service we would have to respect.

As it turns out, the Church does not ask a whole lot.

'There is an Opening Prayer,' the Reverend Friend explains. 'That is where Father Alan will welcome people. It can be short, and nothing that people should be uncomfortable with.'

He is flicking through a book that he has brought with him, searching for the section that will help us get an idea of what is required. He points at the page detailing the different parts of the funeral Mass. 'Then there is the Liturgy of the Word. There will need to be a reading. I brought with me a number that are quite nice and the Church will accept.'

He produces a sheet that has a list of various readings by different writers, philosophers, poets.

I am surprised, having underestimated the flexibility of the Church when it comes to such things.

'This will be followed by the Liturgy of the Eucharist.'

'Do we have to have communion?' I jump in to ask, feeling guilty doing so. While my Father and Parents-in-Law might expect it, I believe my Brother and his friends would not.

'No, Communion is not necessary for a Funeral Mass,' he reassures me. 'But you might like to have presentation of gifts?' He pauses, looking at each of us in turn.

I don't hesitate.

'Yes, yes of course, that would be lovely.' Already I am thinking of my Brother's guitar, his chess board, some art. The list could be endless.

'Then there is the Prayer of Commendation,' he says. 'This is necessary. This is where the priest commends the deceased into the hands of the Lord. And lastly there is the Farewell.'

'Right, so if we have that covered,' my Husband says, 'we can more or less fit in readings and music in around that?'

'Well a lot would depend on Father Alan, but I get the feeling from what I know of him that he will be fairly amenable to your ideas.'

'That's great. Now that I know what is necessary, I feel I have some flexibility to talk to him about the rest.' My Husband shuffles his notes together. 'Thanks.' He pauses, thinking about something: 'I was wondering would you do the reading for us?'

I smile, thinking this is a great idea. And better yet, my Mother likes the Reverend Friend, having spent a week in his and his wife's company as part of a European Twinning vacation. I think my Mother would approve. My Sister-in-Law, I am guessing, won't understand the significance.

If our friend is surprised to be asked, he doesn't show it.

It is the small things that can matter all of a sudden.

Being the age I am, at a stage of certain follicle management, once a month I choose to endure the brief agony of waxing, zapping, and threading, so that for a short while at least I can feel comfortable in myself. My usual appointment is not due for another week, but with the week that is in it I become acutely aware of all the close physical contact I am going to have with all the meeting and greeting and consoling of well-wishers. God forbid I might spike someone with one of my blunted strays on cheek or chin. And so it is a priority for me to get an appointment at the beautician's for the next day.

There is nothing like playing the dead card to get a beauty appointment. Same goes with the hairdressers.

Of course, there will be those who would criticise me for getting the hair and waxing done when my Brother has just died. So be it. But there is a lot to be said for getting away and escaping the masses, even family, by enduring some physical pain and pleasure in the one day.

As I said, we all handle grief differently. This is my way.

My Father's focus is on the windows.

We couldn't possibly have people up for the Wake looking through the salt-splattered windows following recent storms. My Mother rolls her eyes when my Father suggests it, and this on its own is an anomaly. She hates dirty windows.

We are certainly not ourselves as we process death.

An argument ensues about the windows, and the task of booking a cleaner becomes the sore point. To save peace, I intervene and ring the window cleaner there and then. I play the dead card then too. He is booked and confirmed for the following morning. Everyone happy. Almost.

We are in my Brother's house. My Mother, my Sister and I. We need to pick out his final outfit. Our footsteps appear to thunder across his yellowed pine floor in the silence of his lifeless machines. We go through his various cupboards. I feel a comfort being in this quiet space. His essence still lingers in the air. How to describe it? My Brother was not a sweater. Even in his mobile days he did not perspire. It was as if his body reserved every droplet to oil his joints and fuel his weakening muscles. Even when he went through his 'roach' days in the old Winstanley shoe factory in Dublin. Hanging with the band unwashed and living in unnecessary squalor, he would cast his five-day-worn socks at me when I visited, demanding I smell them as proof of his uniqueness. A great pride in his lack of smell. A rarity all on its own. Here now in the house I suck at the air, attempting to find him in the floating dust mites that dance on the window's light rays. There is a hint of it yet. His fragrance of vanilla tinged with salt. It clings to the smell of wood and dry heat, permeated by his Wife's chilli spice and deep-fry oil. I close my eyes and imagine he is here still, sleeping in the next room. But this is a false image as it lacks the sounds that would usually go with it. Where is the hum of his bed, the whoosh of his breathing mask, the background mumblings of the TV or music that always accompanied his slumber?

'Should we put him in a suit?' my Mother asks.

'No,' I say firmly. 'He never liked suits. 'Put him in a tee. He loved his tees.'

'Yes,' agrees my Sister, 'with one of his trendy jackets. His green one.' She roots through his wardrobe.

'What trousers?' my Mother asks.

'What about his fat pants?' I ask, referring to the special trousers designed for the overweight and disabled who need quick easy access. It has a large square flap at the front with Velcro for a zipper.

'No,' my Sister says. 'He was more comfortable in his pyjamas.'

She is right. My Brother's preference was his wacky old-man paisley pyjamas, choosing only to wear his fat pants if he had to be social for visitors or go out somewhere. She rifles through his collection, picking out a pair that will complement the jacket.

'We can't put pyjamas on him,' my Mother says, unconvincingly.

'Sure no one need see,' I say. 'The undertakers can cover up that bit of him. Hide his belly.'

'Don't forget his cap and scarf,' my Sister adds. 'And his man-bag.'

'We should include some hash,' my Sister giggles. I laugh with her. A shared memory triggered.

'We must make sure to include some Dulcolax,' I snigger.

We are both laughing at ourselves.

'Girls!' my Mother checks us.

We stop laughing and look straight-faced at her.

'We can add all that later.' She doesn't bat an eye. 'The undertaker just needs the clothes they will put on him for now.'

My Sister and I laugh again. My Mother, hard as nails but ever complicit in the comfort of my Brother. Even during his alternative living. Even in the after-life.

Content with the makings of his final outfit, we leave my Brother's house and make our way over the Bridge of Woe to the main house.

'I don't think we can do the boots and the umbrella,' my Mother says out of the blue.

I feel my innards twist within me. Somewhere low and deep. Like my cloud has slumped downwards with the weight of chains.

'I mean I know what Fergus was trying to do, but I don't think we should do it.'

'Yeah Lyd,' my Sister walks besides my Mother. 'I can see the funny side of it but I'm thinking what Li's reaction will be, what others will think.'

I tell myself to remain calm. But I am determined. 'We needn't have them in the church for the celebration. Just the Wake, like,' I suggest.

'Li will think we are mad,' my Sister adds.

We have reached the mid-way point between the two houses. Passing beside what was my Brother's music studio, I know I have only a brief moment to convince them. I need to have them on my side if I am to win my Father over. And I need to do it before we reach the sanctuary of the main house. Where they will split and the subject will be buried under a mound of other suggestions.

'Li already knew Fergus was mad,' I say light heartedly. 'I don't think she will be surprised at all. Anyway, no doubt Ferg told her all about his wishes already.'

'I dunno,' my Sister says dismissively and walking ahead makes her way head down into the drizzle that has begun to flow.

I stop walking and look to my Mother, who pauses with me.

'Mom, Fergus never asked me to do something important for him. Yes, I did his books and admin and paper work. Fetched things. Did that sort of stuff. But this was something special he asked of me. His final wishes. That's why he signed it.'

Here I gulp because I do not want to cry and lose control and lose sight of the message I am trying to impart.

'He trusted me to get this done for him.'

My face is wet. I am hoping my tears blend in with the soft rain that clings to my cheeks. My Mother stands listening. Processing. Squinting.

'It's important to me that I do this for him. For me.'

My Mother nods silently and we both take up our step again towards the big house, heads bent into the weight of it all.

'Hey there, it's me.'

'Hello pet. How are you doing? I am so sorry…' I hear a lump form in the back of my Writing Friend's throat.

'I know, I know.' I take a breath. Inject some mirth in my voice. 'Listen, I have an unusual favour to ask.'

'Shout,' she says. 'Anything.'

'It's kind of an odd one,' I start. 'It's to do with the arrangements.'

'Okay...'

'You know we don't do anything by halves.'

I hear her laugh down the phone.

'Ferg left me with some instructions, and I figure you're the woman for the job.'

'Okay,' she repeats, this time with an air of wariness about her.

'I need to arrange to have Ferg's boots attached to his coffin.'

'What?' I think she thinks she misheard me.

'And an umbrella.' I am smiling down the phone at how ridiculous it sounds.

'And smiley faces.'

My Writing Friend is laughing.

'Brilliant,' she says, 'Trust Fergus to come up with that.' She is cry-laughing now.

I am too.

'Yes. You see that's exactly what he wanted,' I explain. 'He wanted people to laugh on seeing him in the coffin. With his boots sticking out. And the umbrella. Not crying and being all sad.'

'Okay,' she says again. 'Yes, of course.' She coughs. Pulling up her professional side. Switching on. We are in project mode.

'I am not up to much myself,' I say, 'but I figure I can rely on you to organise it. Maybe if you speak to Maria, or Julia,' I offer.

'Julia is away on holidays today. But don't worry, leave it with me.'

'Kym might help,' I suggest. 'She worked a lot with Ferg, on Mrs Freeborn, you know, the orangutan?'

'Yes of course,' she says. 'Okay, so boots. Any boots?'

'No. His own ones,' I clarify. 'He will have a wicker casket, so I'm thinking they could be attached somehow.'

'Yes, yes.'

I visualise her cogs motoring as she thinks through, visualises the set-up herself, how it might work.

'Can I come up at some stage to collect the boots?'

'Yes, of course. And I'll send you an image from the catalogue of the coffin so you can get an idea of what you will be working with.'

'Now tell me a bit more about the umbrella....'

I love this woman. She will select those people she in turn trusts, and through their imagination and West Cork magic they will work it. For the love of my Brother, for me. It will be so.

'There is a caveat,' I warn.

'Okay.' My friend of a former legal life is listening.

'We're not sure if Li knows yet about Ferg's wishes and so we don't know what her reaction will be. I figure get the ball rolling on it and set it up so we can go with it, or not, as the case may be. You know?'

'That's fine,' she says. 'Leave it with me. If it suits, I might call up later and collect the boots?'

'Yes, of course,' I say, already wondering where his boots are and if I can get them out without causing any emotional disturbance.

'I will leave them at the porch of his house,' I say. 'He won't be there yet. The undertakers will be delivering him tomorrow. You can pick them up in the hall. The front door will be open.'

'Sure.'

'Don't call into Mom and Dad. They are not really up to visitors yet.'

'No worries. I'll be in and out and no one will notice.'

The cumulus within me lifts a bit and I feel my heart swell some. Fresh oxygenated blood rushes in and I am feeling something else. A sense of satisfaction? A smidge of happiness? Guilt tries to push up from that dark place in my stomach to shove the happiness away but I won't let it. I will allow this feeling of light push through.

I make a promise to myself there and then to allow any happiness filter in where it fits. I will allow that lightness of being to be. No doubt great sadness is yet to come, but where there is light, I will let it be.

Just be.

Be.

Don't Go Down

Through the glass I can see the stars.
Ya I was born with a wishing heart.
No matter what life brings I won't let it rattle me.
When I'm up against a turning tide,
And everything starts to twist inside,
Won't go down on my knees
Gonna let it ride over me.
Ahmmmm!

When life has got me up against the ropes.
It's raining punches there's nowhere to go.
I'm gonna float like a butterfly and sting like a bee.

When I'm tangled in the mess of things
And all the bullshit that living brings.
Won't go down on my knees gonna let it ride over me

Ahmmm.

Through the glass I can see the stars.
Ya I was born with a wishing heart.
No matter what life brings I won't let it rattle me.

When I'm tangled in the mess of things
And all the bullshit that living brings.
Won't go down on my knees gonna let it ride over me.

For a man who could not walk, my Brother wore a pair of boots that bore the markings of many of life's miles. Yet turn them over and the soles are as new and unworn as the day they were purchased.

My Brother's boots are a good metaphor of how he lived. Mountain boots. Hard core, designed for trekkers, with reinforced toe, thick soles, high lace ups, ankle and arch supporting. At first glance, his are fit for recycling. Worn, ripped, scuffed, discoloured, seams threadless. Friction and weathering has left the once black shiny leather dull, faded, and grey. Almost white in places. 'Will-do' laces strain on the Northwest hooks to keep some order on the otherwise as-good-as-fit-for-the-bin size tens. Years of rubbing off his chair wheels have the upper outsoles scuffed and threadbare. Seams ripped and thinned so much in places that they curl back on themselves as if grinning at the world. Droplets of paint dot the grey toes here and there because of his years of artwork. Red, blues, greens: a unique signature of cosmic-like splodges symbolic of his effervescent universe.

'A man without boots feels sorry for himself until he meets the man without feet.'

Anyone who knew my Brother, knew his boots. They may not have chosen to walk in them but would have been honoured to have been asked.

Facebook is awash with postings. There is an endless reel of sympathy, condolence, shock, loss, and reach-outs. Many are friends, a lot are fans, some are strangers.

I find solace in the streams of consciousness that flow. A range of my Brother's images pop up in the running statuses. Some are familiar, others are photos I have not seen in many years. I smile at these and appreciate the effort someone made to find their old photo albums, search for images of my Brother and copy and paste them to their status for sharing. Comments accompany these sometimes funny images and my Sister and I flag the ones that either of us might have missed. My Mother, a technophobe, is happy to look at the ones we have filtered to share, passing our respective iPads to her for viewing.

'Look, this one already has eighty-three likes,' my Sister says.

'Did you see the one with the interview?' I ask.

'The RTE one, with David whatshisname?' my Sister asks.

'No, the one in front of the piano – it's not the radio recording. Another one, a live documentary.' I am sliding through my profile status trying to pull it up again. 'I think it is the Nationwide one.'

Finding it, I see a thinner version of my Brother. 'It's amazing how flexible he was even then,' I say, finding the piece and turning my iPad towards my Sister.

'Oh yeah,' she says. 'I watched that one last night.'

'I couldn't watch all of it,' I say. 'Too much for me. But I can't get over the difference in him. I mean even his shoulders and neck movement are so much more animated.'

I look down at the paused image. His steel blue eyes looking back at me. His expression frozen in a serious business-like state. Eyebrows raised. Eyes hooked on the camera. Mouth held in a crescent, verging on a smile. Strong chin, straight nose. Handsome. I visualise him now. The contrast. At least how he was earlier this week. Alive. So different.

His face swollen, jowly, extra chins, stubble. Eyes clouded, misty almost. Like a fog had come in from the Fastnet, snuck in around his head, clung to the back of his eyes and slowed down his brain.

'God, he really had got in a bad way,' I say. It is a sad reality. I was too close to notice his demise, seeing him on an almost daily basis. No gap to notice a difference. *'There's the man that ate Fergus O' Farrell,'* a friend had joked having not seen him in a while. If he had lived, what quality of life would it have been? The cloud in me shifts, thins and spreads, creeping in around my chest cavity, clinging to my heart, my lungs and stomach.

Lingers.

Stratocumulus.

OVERLOAD: A SECRET

A thing can eat away at a person.
Sometimes it's the knowing.
Sometimes it's what you don't know.
But one thing's for sure: once you know a
thing, you can't unknow it.

'You see,' my Sister says, 'didn't I say she would come straight down?'

It is after 9pm and my Brother's Original Band Member Friend in Dublin has confirmed that he will meet my Brother's wife and her son at the airport and come straight to the house.

'They'll drive through the night,' my Father explains.

'God, they'll be exhausted,' I say. Jet lag on top of grief and the five-hour drive. 'Fair play to James.'

We all take stock. It is unsaid, but we all know that everything will change with the arrival of my Sister-in-Law.

My Brother liked to describe her as his 'controlled nuclear explosion'. In one of his songs, she is his 'busy bee'. None of us really know what to expect when she arrives. Except my Sister. She believes there will be chaos. That our Sister-in-Law will want to go directly to my Brother who is in the process of being prepared in the undertakers. *Prepared.* Where he will be sprayed, sliced, pierced, pickled, trussed, trimmed, creamed, waxed, painted, rouged, and neatly dressed. Not due to return home till Thursday mid-morning.

'Well, she'll just have to wait,' my Mother says.

'Ah no, she'll be exhausted,' my diplomatic Father says. 'She'll want to go straight to bed.'

'Well, there is no point in waiting up for them,' my Mother says. I look at her now. She looks tired. Together but tired. Like she herself has jet lag and Greenwich Mean Time hasn't caught up with her yet.

'Well, I'm not going to bed,' my Sister announces.

'Yeah, I'll wait up for her too,' I offer. 'I think some of us have to be up to greet them.'

I am in bed and asleep within the hour.

It is a restless sleep. Like the ones I used to have in boarding school the night before travel, anxious I might miss the bus or train. Like the night before exams, worried that I might sleep through the alarm. Or when I was a new mother half sleeping for fear of missing my newborn's mewling. But there is an added weight on my mind now and it bites at my conscience. Despite setting my phone alarm, my body clock jerks me awake. Glancing at my screen I see it is after 2am. I get out of bed and stagger sleepily downstairs, supposing that arrivals were due any time now.

There is a disturbance in the sitting room, and for a moment I think it is the television. Then I remember that is where my Sister is sleeping, taking to the couch so she can have the TV for company in order to be able to drift off to sleep. It is my Sister I hear, bawling. I step into the room and find her perched on the side of the couch bent over. Her head is in her hands and she is rocking her body in rhythm to each wave of grief that is rolled out from deep within her. I am at her side in an instant and bend over her, wrapping myself around her and I take up her rhythm. Unspeaking, she slows some and we rock together until she is spent. Sitting up, she takes a drink from her bottled water. There is no need for words. Secrets shared don't need words.

'What time is it?' she asks hoarsely.

'Must be after half two,' I guess.

Timing is perfect as I hear one of the dogs bark an alert that someone is outside. Opening the front door, I look across the Bridge of Woe to see the red tail-lights of a car.

'They're here,' I call back towards the sitting room.

My Sister comes out wiping her face and we both scurry down towards the hazy red glow. Our movement ignites the spotlight at the studio and we are lit up while the arrivals are plunged into darkness again. I can just make out some movement around the car and recognise the tall gangly form of my Brother's Original Band Member Friend and instinctively step into him. I am dwarfed by his body and limbs as he bends over to hug me. This is the first of many such meetings I am going to have over the next few days and there is no pausing the clock now. It ticks and tocks, pushing forward, turning the page on the next chapter of our lives.

My Sister greets our Step-Nephew first as our Sister-in-Law has yet to disentangle from the car. I step around the hugging pair and time it to be on the other side for my Sister-in-Law when she finally emerges and straightens herself.

'Li,' I say and take her in my arms. Like my Mother, my Sister-in-Law has never been a natural hugger. I understand it is not the Chinese way. Public displays of affection, awkward and avoided. Now she makes an effort to respond by pressing her arms into my back.

'Why you wake?' she says into my ear. 'Too late. You go to bed.' Her voice sounds tired, strained but gentle.

'We wanted to greet you, Li,' I explain.

She breaks away from me and, laden with her many hand-held plastic bags, she steps towards my Sister who is coming at us now. I have stepped round to hug my Step-Nephew. His hug is more natural, yet with a respectful reserve that his culture hasn't fully knocked out of him. We don't say anything. I can't because of the lump that has grown knobbly in the back of my throat, and if I try and talk I will just burst into tears. I do not want to embarrass either of our Chinese relatives with a raw show of Irish keening. It is too soon for that. They will see plenty of it over the next week.

'James, you're upstairs in the double room,' I explain as he unpacks the car. My Step-Nephew is helping his mom with bags. I hug my cardigan around myself as the cold night drizzle whips around us. He thanks me, and feeling there is no more to be done, I remember my Father's last instructions.

'Oh, there is some Chinese takeaway by the microwave if ye are hungry, and some beers in the fridge.' My ever-caring Father had remembered how his daughter-in-law is always famished after travelling from a trip abroad.

Calling out goodnight, I turn and make my way across to the main house. My Sister follows after me. I sense she is stiff with upset, her face pulled as if in a vice. I am not sure if it is from grief at meeting them, or anger, I cannot tell. The black night's drizzle is distorting my perception. I hold my tongue, knowing that she will soon let me know which it is.

It is morning and my Mother is sat at her desk digesting her morning coffee and cigarette, asking how the arrival went. We are all a bit groggy. I am feeling somewhat nauseous, be it from too little sleep, second-hand smoke, and dehydration from weeping.

'Oh, it was fine,' I offer. 'They arrived sometime before three.'

My Sister lights up her own cigarette and launches into her version of events. She describes a scene of my Sister-in-Law's impatience at us having waited up. Of short quips and dismissive gestures. Of an overall lack of appreciation. I am surprised at her account. I attempt to counter-argue, fearful of getting a reprimand.

'Ah no, it wasn't like that,' I shake my head at my Mother. 'Li was tired, not cross. Embarrassed by us staying up to greet them even.'

My Sister is not convinced. My Mother doesn't comment. She looks from one of us to the other and then changes the subject by asking again what time my Brother is due home. I stand and go to put on the kettle, choosing silence over discussion. My Sister is back scrolling through her iPad, commenting on new likes and posts.

My Sister and I are opposites. We take different views of the world. My Brother was our middle-man. We used to bounce things off each other. He and I. Test the waters as such before putting it to the rest of the family. My siblings were two halves. But he and I could talk to each other when we needed to vent or criticise or analyse those close to us, without it ending in an argument or a screaming match. It was something that I will miss about him. For now though, a gentle breeze is blowing. A South Westerly. Sisterly. And cumulonimbus clouds are gathering.

We are now living in a parallel world to the norm. Those that rise go to work, pay bills, make calls, stress over meetings and deals to be done, scream at kids, prepare dinner, do laundry. Our world is consumed with pockets of the extraordinary: what happens next, the pending Wake and funeral.

Everything else is a void.

A black hole.

Time revolves around two pivotal points on our virtual timepiece.

The Wake, planned for Christ's hour on Friday. And the funeral, on Saturday at five.

I flit between my Mother's kitchen, my Brother's house, the big room and bedroom. It is my new world. My head is wrecked with overthinking how my Brother died and processing our loss.

I function. I barely parent. My Son is gifted a freedom to all devices, television and treat requests. 'Yes, you can' has become my standard response. My teen daughters retreat into their world of Facebook, Snapchat, and Instagram.

Thanks to my local Old-School Buddy and her co-ordination of generous neighbours and woman friends, we do not have to plan meals or cook. My Husband, my Brother-in-Law, and my Father are busily distracted with planning, phone calls, and funeral business.

I float within the cumulus that now surrounds the entire household. Unable to make any intelligent independent decisions, I am limited to performing functionary roles and an ability to answer only closed questions. I am catatonic-like. Drifting as a zombie, with a biomass of cerebral mush.

'So sorry to hear about Fergus.'

I am at the village petrol station and turn to face a Commiserator.

'Thank you,' I say, not at all grateful for their sympathy.

'Was he sick?'the Commiserator asks.

'No,' I say. 'Not this time anyway.'

'It was unexpected?' the Commiserator prods. The death notice quoted back to me.

'Yes.' My mind's eye sees my Brother's face. If only they knew. 'Yes, yes it was.'

'What happened?' they have the cheek to ask.

'Shortness of breath,' I say. It is not a lie.

The sympathy face is pulled. I nod. They nod.

'It was quick,' I say, trying to convince myself.

'A good way to go,' they say.

Hah.

Inside I am screaming.

'Yes,' I say aloud.

'God rest him,' they say.

'Yes,' I say, anxious to be on my way, moving to the side to get around them.

This conversation, or variations of it, are repeated again and again. For those that are closer in my circle a little more detail is given.

'We're not sure.' The truth knocks around inside my head. 'His lungs gave out or something.'

'He got into difficulty breathing.' It is a partial truth. 'Managed to call 999 himself. The Home Help found him, and knowing there was something wrong, went up for Mom.' I might include for added drama, 'Did you know that Home Help aren't trained for CPR?'

The sympathy nod, eyebrows narrowed.

'By the time they came back down the ambulance had arrived.' At least that is one of my Mother's versions. Or the other, 'Mom was with him when the crew arrived.' Or another, 'She was just at the door when the crew pushed past her.'

'That was quick,' some might say.

'Yes it was a fast turnaround,' I usually answer.

But what of those minutes in between?

'They brought him to Bantry, but I think he had gone by then.'

The guilt of it.

More nodding. Sometimes there is an intake of breath.

'They had a heartbeat back by then so they had to keep going,' I might explain, adding, 'I think that was just the adrenaline they gave him though.' That was my Mother's explanation for it anyway. 'Mom was with him.' That much is true.

'He never regained consciousness but was faintly breathing in the hospital. She was with him, talking to him, holding him up to the last.' There is always that hope in what they say about hearing – that it is the last to go.

With the re-telling of the story I have become strong enough not to cry at this point. But the listener is usually moved. Their face screws up. The more emotional ones will have tears in their eyes. But all of them have a certain sense about them, as if that is enough for them, as if they are satisfied. The good end. His Mother with him.

'First to see him into the world,' I say. 'Last to see him out.'

It is a borrowed quote from an earlier telling when a friend used the punch line. I have used it thereafter for any new private audience, doing an Oscar Wilde on it. Rehearsed lines, achieving a self-centred satisfied result. It is street theatrics.

You asked. I shall tell.

But not the Secret bit.

No one must know about that.

Night sleeps are broken now.

As if on watch, my body wakes at three or four-hour intervals. There is no point tossing and turning, I will only disturb my Husband. Having experienced the same during late stages of pregnancy, I acquiesce to this new pattern, knowing that sleep will catch up on me later. For now, I get up and go downstairs to the kitchen to make a cup of herbal tea.

My Sister is there ahead of me sitting in her kaftan at the breakfast room round table, with her iPad and fags and plastic bottle of water nearby. My Sister-in-Law sits opposite her, still wearing her outdoor coat, hovering on the edge of the kitchen chair, leaning in towards my Sister. Her head is tilted as she absorbs what my Sister tells her. My Sister-in-Law looks exhausted from both grief and jet-lag; her face is yellowed, and dark puffy bags hang under her bloodshot eyes.

I have interrupted an animated conversation. It sounds like an interrogation. I can hear the anguish and impatience in my Sister's answers.

'No Li, not his heart,' my Sister says, sighing. 'His heart good.'

'Yes, yes,' my Sister-in-Law nods her head in agreement, 'his heart good, strong.' She tuts. 'Strong heart.' She repeats, thumping her own chest.

'We don't know exactly what happened,' my Sister continues. 'We think his lung muscles stop working.' She is reverting to broken banter as if it might make it easier to understand.

My Sister glances up at me. I blink, say nothing. Turning towards the coffee dock, I put on the kettle. I am out of sight now, still within earshot. I take a deep breath. A person cannot un-know something, and I wonder will my Sister hide this well enough.

I realise that while we presume to know my Sister-in-Law, I never considered that she might do the same of us. Could she know that my Sister is lying?

I turn back towards the small round table and sit. We are the three witches – brooding over a cauldron.

'He ring ambulance himself?' my Sister-in-Law asks.

'Yes, Li.' My Sister takes a pull of her cigarette, adding to the cloud hovering over the table.

'He speak with Mama around half twelve and then he call Home Help,' my Sister says. 'They not come till one, so Ferg decide to stay in bed. Do medicine before she come.'

The kettle clicks off from boiling, and I get up again to go through the motions, slowly, of getting a camomile tea from the adjoining pantry, taking a mug from the cupboard and putting in the bag and hot water. All the time listening to my Sister account for my Brother's last few moments.

'He called the ambulance himself,' my Sister repeats.

'Why no call Mama?'

'I don't know, Li. Mum have no missed calls,' she says truthfully.

Squeezing my tea bag and laying it on the draining board, I return with my comfort crutch to the table.

'The hospital said he was on the 999 call for sixteen minutes,' I add, sitting.

'What he say?'

'We don't know Li,' I say, sadly looking at my Sister over the lip of my cup.

'Can we get tape?'

I almost gag and move the cup away from my mouth. My head whirls with the idea and images of drama movies, reality shows and the horror of playbacks. Does she know what she is asking?

But it is not for me to decide. I am not his wife who wants answers. She who may be suffering the guilt of having left him to go travelling to China for three weeks.

'He promise me he no die when I go China,' she says tearfully, as if reading my mind.

My heart breaks for her. And then I feel anger. How arrogant, or naive, or love-struck of my Brother to say such a thing to his wife. Who are any of us to make such promises?

He should have known better.

Want to make God laugh? Tell him your plans.

'Li, I have a photo.'

She looks up at me through clouded eyes.

'From when he was in hospital.' I am looking up my phone for the photos I took when my Brother was still freshly dead, blood congealing. I have no idea of what my Sister-in-Law's reaction will be but feel the distraction might be worth it.

'Do you want to see?'

Her face is scrunched up in puzzlement as she moves across the room to look over my shoulder at my phone.

'I took this very shortly after he died,' I explain.

'Bali-amah!' she exclaims. Whisking the phone out of my hand she tilts it to get a better focus on the picture and then uses her thumb and fingertip to enlarge the screen, scanning over it.

'Ai-ya,' she says, as she stamps her foot. For a fraction of a second I think she is disgusted and then as quickly realise that she is delighted. She moves the viewer around the close up of my Brother's face, around his cheek, his chin, his ear.

'Oh thank you, thank you.' My Sister-in-Law is bowing and beaming at me. I look over to my Sister who looks on incredulous.

'I thought you might like to see him before...to see him before he was prepared,' I explain.

She is not listening to me really. Her face is transfixed. Like a child in front of their favourite TV show, where no other sound or voice will infiltrate their world of fiction. Only this time, it is her world of fact, and she is seeing her husband as she might have seen him if she were to have been here herself. At least as close as she could be to the moment. There is no other way she can claw back that time, but through the photo she is there with him in the hospital. Her face softens as she hunches over the small screen and magnifies my Brother's face. To see his whiskers, his blue tinged lips, his resting hands, his bent-up knees. I feel as if I am intruding as she sits and tuts, her fingers sliding around the small screen.

'You send me?' she asks, looking up through wet eyes.

'Yes, of course.' I say. She has handed me back the phone and watches me eagerly, waiting. I complete the task asked, feeling chuffed that my macabre deed back at the hospital has paid off.

THURSDAY

February 4

I wake with a jolt. I cannot breathe. My throat is restricted. I attempt to inhale but it is as if I am in a vacuum. I am suffocating. Sitting up in the bed, I swing my legs over the side. My hands grip the mattress and I lean into the darkness, gasping for air. My Husband is woken by my sucking noises and reaches over the bed to my side. I keep gulping but the air won't go past my throat. I am terrified. I feel my diaphragm spasm as if it is trying to kick-start.

My Husband crawls to me and commands me to breathe. 'It is a panic attack,' he explains, calmly but firmly.

Again I suck. My eyes are gone too big in my head and I feel them bulge against my eye sockets. I turn staring at him, beseeching him to do something. My strength is waning. I feel as if I am slipping downward into a deathly hold. I am terrified that I am being called away by some greater being. I don't want to go.

'Breathe,' he commands again. 'The air is there. You are taking it in.' He rubs my back. Hugs me loosely towards him. I feel my chest release. Open. Air rushes in. My chest heaves. My eyes slide back into position. Panting now. I burst into tears and fold. My Husband cradles me.

'It's okay,' he soothes. 'It was just a panic attack. You're okay.'

I let the tears flow and curl into a foetus position on the bed. My Husband spoons me and, reaching down, pulls the duvet around us both. He wraps his arms around me, nuzzling his face into the back of my neck. He breathes slowly, silently encouraging me to match his rhythm. I pace my breath to his but can only think of my Brother. What was his horror? A horror now eating away inside of me. And so I decide I have to share it. I will share the horror of it. We are husband and wife. More than that. We are best friends after all. We share everything.

My Brother has come home to us.

He is to be waked in his own space surrounded by his things and looking out at the view that was his kingdom at the last. His *Wan Xiang* – the Chinese name chosen with his wife for his music publishing company. I understand that when translated it can either mean a high office with a thousand views or, if said with a certain intonation, a thousand elephants. Both are appropriate.

I did not witness my Sister-in-Law welcome him home. I chose not to go down, to give her and her son some space. It will be their first time to see their loved one since last seeing him alive. I cannot imagine the heartache for them.

Yet, it is she that seeks me in my Mother's house, and I am taken aback that she has done so.

'You know I very happy you take this photo.'

She has pulled up the image of my Brother on her phone, tutting again as she manipulates her fingers to expand the image, get a close- up of his face. 'It very important to see after he die.' She leans into me. 'You see here. Blue.' She has pulled up a close-up of where his chin meets his ear.

My stomach lurches. Does she suspect something?

'You think he sick?' She looks up from the phone directly into my eyes.

'No, Li. He definitely wasn't sick.' At least I am being honest with her. 'Was he sick when you left?' I ask in an attempt to clear her head of any misgivings.

'No,' she declares, stamping her foot, as if I might have insulted her that she would go away when he was sick. 'No sick.'

'Exactly. He wasn't,' I say, agreeing vehemently. 'You left when he was in good health.' I soften my tone. 'He did not get sick in the two days.'

I shake my head. 'We don't know for sure exactly what happened.'

I try not to stare at her, balance looking at her directly but not for too long – isn't that what they say about body language? The liars will over-stare. I shuffle my feet under the table.

She goes quiet, thinking, and then tilting her head sideways she looks up at me from the corner of her eye. Serious looking. 'Do you think he take something?'

What! Take something? Does she actually think he might have committed suicide? Taken his own life? It had never dawned on me to think it. That she might think it. And then, of course, if he was healthy, how did he die? And then my mind races. Do others think he might have taken his own life too? No! Shame. Shame on them if they do.

And I think back to conversations my Brother and I had over the years when he lost two friends by their own hand. The anger he felt when they died. How two of my Sister's husband's nephews had taken their own lives within six months of each other, aged 16 and 21. The family grief and shock as a result of that. My Brother's own thoughts on the matter. That those who had fit, able bodies, where life had so much to offer them, should choose to end it. How angry that made him.

But that was a few years ago when he had yet to begin lose control of his own body. When the medication had not yet started to mess with his mind. When the lack of oxygen to his head hadn't begun to affect his brain. When he was still able to drink alcohol for the joy of it, eat from a plate sitting upright. Could control his bowel movements. Even still, I am confident that he had not chosen to take his own life, not yet.

'No, Li,' I say firmly. 'He didn't take his own life.' And I can say this with complete and utter honesty. I cannot tell her why I know this. Should I? It is not my secret to tell. Or is it? I am torn. What is that old cliché? *What you don't know, won't hurt you?* I made a promise to my Father. I will not be the one to tell her. That is my Father's right. My Father's burden.

She is looking back at the image. 'Why blue here and here?' she asks, pointing out the blue tinge again and where there looks like some bruising on his face.

'Maybe it is from when he struggled in the bed. You know trying to breathe?' I suggest. At least this much could be true. That my Brother got into difficulty, couldn't breathe. 'We think his lung stopped working.' Which isn't really a lie. 'And when he couldn't breathe he try to take off mask.'

I have reverted to broken banter, swivelling my head back and forth to imitate what action he might have taken on his bed. Unable to lift his own arms, he would have had to use friction, wriggling his head against the pillow to get the encumbering mask off his face. I am getting upset at the thought of it. Tears brim my eyes.

'His head moving might have bruised his neck and cheek, you know, where the straps were.' I stroke my own wet warm cheek to show the line of the mask. She nods back at me, thinking. Processing. She is tutting again.

'You know, in China we can see from body how die.' She pauses. 'Body tell us.' She looks at me and then at the photo again. 'This photo very important to me. Thank you sooo much,' she says again, reaching out for my arm, squeezing firmly. 'I love,' she says.

It is a genuine appreciation of giving her something special. She leaves the room again in a flurry, and I rub my arm where it is still throbbing from her grip.

I am wary of crossing my Brother's sitting room to the conservatory, knowing he is laid out there.

There beyond the double glass doors. His own song is playing in the background.

Treading gently, I follow the music that hums from the room and step into its *Wan Xiang* light. There in the centre lies my dead Brother. His nose and cheek all that I can see from here, his face peeping from within the pine-coloured wicker casket. I step in a little closer. I remind myself that I have already seen him dead. And hope that he still looks like himself.

And he does. More so, he looks great. Lying there looking dapper in his khaki-green mod bomber jacket and black tee showing just at the collar. And his sunglasses.

The make-up artist has done a wonderful job, sticking to her remit. He is looking exactly like himself. A fine head of hair on him looking healthy and thick. Clean shaven save the sculpted dark handlebar moustache he had been working hard on to achieve.

'Give them something to look at on my face. Distract them from my belly,' he had said to justify it. Bless him.

Here he is now laid out, facing west to watch the sun set over Schull harbour. With his handlebar 'tache.

I am impressed with the wicker casket. There is an air of comfort about it. Informal. Dare I suggest, cosy. The morticians have left it fully open, save the cream linen fringe that skirts the edge and, as expected, hides my Brother's lower half. Hides his paisley PJs. Only from his waist up is exposed. As instructed, they have dressed him in his jacket, tee, and scarf. They have left his cap, casually lain, to the side. It is as if he has just arrived, or is getting ready to go. *Here's your hat, what's your hurry.*

His man purse, the black leather pouch that accompanied him everywhere, sits on his chest, the strap around his jowly neck. His soft gentle hands grasp each other, not in prayer but one hand holding his wrist as he was wont to do when lying in his bed. The sunglasses give some added character, gifted by my Mother to him a few weeks ago at Christmas. Big enough to fit the inherited wide O'Farrell head, and with lenses designed to wrap around enough so they don't let any glare in.

My Brother, to all intents and purposes, looks like a true rock-n-roller or Gringo Pimp. He would be delighted with either.

It is all part of the plan to make people laugh. But in a good way.

The Fergus way.

I smile to myself. What will he look like with the boots and umbrella?

They have been signed off. I got the go ahead. I reached out to my Step-Nephew to translate and explain my Brother's wishes to my Sister-in-Law. Once I had her on board, sure there was no going back. My Sister-in-Law was happy to go along, suggested using his good boots as part of his final wish installation, but I rejected those.

'He wore the old ones all the time, Li. They were his favourite. Most comfortable.'

'Ah, yes.'

'The good ones are not the true him. He lived his life wearing the old boots.'

She nods her head. Understanding. Agreeing.

I have received confirmation from my Writing Friend that she has a team working on the various props. They will arrive Friday morning to set him up. For now, it is just us. His family. Our last few hours with him alone. We all take different turns to be with him. My Sister stays throughout. She will not leave his side. As when they were kids and teens and even into adulthood. She was his loyal constant companion. He was her best friend.

He is home only hours when a couple, the first of the mourners arrive.

My Mother is furious. The Wake is not scheduled till tomorrow. And even that is private, reserved for family and close friends. Today is supposed to be just for us.

'Who are they?' my Mother demands through clenched teeth as my Father welcomes them in to offer a drink.

Catching up with my Father in the kitchen, the woman hands over her two plates of sandwiches, offers her condolences and accepts the glass of whiskey from him.

'We weren't expecting people till tomorrow,' my Mother almost snarls as she moves to sit at her desk and lights a cigarette.

'Sorry, we're a day early,' the man starts guiltily. 'We have to go away for a few days and won't be here tomorrow or for the funeral.' He sips the whiskey that has been handed to him.

'We're all gutted,' the woman says, explaining that her brother was in bits when he heard the news.

It takes me a moment to connect the dots. Their brother who emigrated a few years back, a friend of my Brother back in the day.

'He is devastated to not be here,' she continues.

'Of course,' my Father says, automatically.

'Come down and see him,' my Father says, nodding in the direction of my Brother's house. He leaves the kitchen with the plates of sandwiches, the two following, whiskey in hand.

'What are they doing here?' my Mother barks again.

I explain to my Mother their connection. We live in a village after all. There are always connections.

'I don't care. They shouldn't be here.'

I am puzzled myself. How do they justify their coming at this time? We haven't had time with my Brother ourselves. Not set up his boots.

'They said they will miss the funeral,' I offer.

'That's their choice,' she says. 'If he meant that much to them, they would stay for the funeral.' She sucks angrily at her cigarette. 'Height of bad manners to show up here today.'

I can't help but agree. We don't always understand local customs. We are blow-ins. Even after thirty years we don't always understand the locals. But all the same, surely respecting the various notices, including the one on the front door, would be good etiquette by anyone's standard.

Following my Mother's instructions and my own curiosity, I make my way down to my Brother.

The two Gate-Crashers are sitting on chairs that have been placed against the walls. My Sister sits nearby, bent towards them, listening quietly, my Father standing nearby. The scene is a strange one for me. For both the man and woman are sincerely upset, moved at the reality of my Brother's death, silent tears flowing down both sets of cheeks. She is sat there, the plate of sandwiches held tilted in one limp wristed hand while she pathetically nibbles at the corner of a sandwich with the other. He is slumped forward, elbows on his knees, round shouldered, with tissue in hand. I am taken aback.

Was their connection to my Brother closer than I had imagined? Was it more than just business and passing on their own brother's condolences? Had I assumed wrongly that they had no right to be here?

Clearly they too are grieving and have lost someone important to them.

The man is talking about my Brother, but I do not hear about the core of their relationship. I am stood at the other side of the casket and close to music speakers that amplify my Brother's music. The song is louder in my ear than the man's gentle confession.

I feel I am intruding. This is their personal time to grieve, to say their goodbye. My Sister and Father are already there to bear witness and so I leave again, across the Bridge of Woe back up to the main house.

My Mother is stil seething. She is smoking a new cigarette.

'They shouldn't be here,' she says again, 'I mean who turns up at a house the day before the announced Wake?' She blows her smoke towards the ceiling.

My Father arrives up unaccompanied. A puzzled look on his face.

'What are they doing here?' my Mother directs her mantra at him.

'I'm not sure,' my Father admits as he pours himself another whiskey. He leans on the counter. He looks shattered, creases anew, waxen skin, shadows under his eyes. The Secret is eating at him too.

'I don't want them here,' my Mother states. My Father looks down into his glass, as if he would dive in and have it swallow him whole.

'I'll go down,' I offer. My Father nods at me.

Back at my Brother's house the Gate-Crashers sit alone silently nibbling their sandwiches. My Sister is not there. Nor is my Sister-in-Law. I presume she is sleeping off the jet lag. I can only think of one reason why my Sister is not with her brother, and that is that she is gone to the loo.

I seize the opportunity and creep in next to them but do not sit. Taking a breath, I bend over so my face is beside theirs, whispering, 'Guys, I hope you don't mind, but I'm going to ask you to leave.'

The woman is more shocked looking than he. Eyes widen. Her sandwich pauses mid-air, her mouth ajar. He looks blankly at me.

'It's just that tonight is the only family night, the Wake tomorrow at three and then the service on Saturday at five.' I can hardly look them in the eye.

The man nods politely and offers quietly 'Of course'. The woman hasn't moved.

'Sorry now, I know it may seem very rude of me but it's just that we weren't expecting anybody till tomorrow, and today, is...well, our only private time with Ferg.'

The man stands and she follows suit.

'Of course,' the man repeats and goes into the explanation of having to go away, missing the funeral. Wanting to pay their respects.

'Of course,' I echo and usher them from the conservatory leading them towards the front door.

'Thank you so much,' I say and scurry away back up to the main house, having abandoned them at their parked car nearby. A cloud of embarrassment lingers between us on the Bridge of Woe.

The big room in my Mother's house is being transformed. My Youngest Daughter has been busy raiding my Father's family archive and has constructed collages of photos of my Brother and us all together over the years. Pinning them to office cork boards and then to cork table mats when she runs out of boards. She is busying being busy. Her mind needing the distraction. Filling it with happy thoughts, not having to endure wailing ones. The Secret is hers too, and I worry that her sixteen years on this planet have not prepared her for carrying it. I try not to dwell on it again and focus on all the images of faces and memories that are on display now.

The big room is a gallery mirroring years of love and happiness, cheerful family times around the evolving musical artist that was my Brother. The photos depict ranges in ages and abilities from birth to running lad, to waddling teen, to wheelchair-bound adult, to obesity. My Brother's fate may have been set since his birth and diagnosis at the age of twelve, but he has witnessed death himself over the years and said goodbye to many family and a few younger friends besides. Thanks to my Father's obsession with preserving family history, his archive houses a treasure trove of photos, letters and mementos. Not just to do with our own family but his before, and those before that, spanning into the last century and beyond. I have a sense of the room becoming a sacred space and of being held by all those that have gone before us and yet to pass. I call on them here now in my Mother's big sitting room, revisiting their images, speaking their names, imaging old times.

It feels as if it is Christmas and the big family table is being prepared, a buffet laid out. Drinks displayed, glasses, cutlery wrapped and crockery stacked. This room will be reserved for the elders, the food and drinks, for those that may be uncomfortable with hanging with the dead, yet still want to pay their respects to the Family. My Mother is delighted with the arrangement. She will not have to cope with the throng, nor the full-on presence of my dead Brother. She will stay in her own space, surrounded by happy memories.

And I realise, that is exactly what it is: a room palpitating with happy memories. How blessed are we as a family, how privileged am I. To have been raised with such love, such contentment. How much of that was the doing of my Parents? The Ball Bearing and the Mallteaser. Nurture. Nature. How much of it my Brother's influence? That life is borrowed. Not ours to keep. No one's is. From the day my Brother was diagnosed, he was the constant silent reminder that death awaits and we must make the most of every day. Our Family knew that this day would come, so we all made the most of every gathering.

I cannot deny the sense of celebration that we are going to experience on his passing. A great reunion of friends and family. There is a smidge of light in my cloud poking through, and I find myself looking forward to the gathering, to seeing so many that we have not seen of late. I might even be excited by it. Feel a little guilty for it. And then push that guilt aside. Guilt is not necessary. I allow myself this happy feeling. His party. His celebration.

My Brother would have wanted it no other way.

FRIDAY

February 5

My Brother's house is all business. And he is at the centre of it.

The living are busy around the dead.

My Sister-in-Law is breaking up newly arrived flower arrangements and placing the flowers in and around her dead husband. She selects the most fragrant ones and places them by his sides and on top of the linen that hides his legs. The wild flowers, his favourites, she breaks up from the bouquet and places them around his head. Adjusting his scarf just so, she cleverly manages to disguise my Brother's spare chins.

Two of his Artist Friends are at the other end of the casket discussing the best method of attaching his boots. False shins covered in thick woollen socks poke out of the boots, which in turn are capped by a small flat wooden shelf. The plan is to invert this so they can attach the shelf part to the casket using plastic ties. They adjust and tilt, manoeuvre and fiddle, brain-storming a way to lock it in place with plastic ties.

Another has brought an umbrella: a dainty child's thing where the original material has been stripped and the skeletal frame expertly covered instead with unbleached linen. It is beautiful in its simplicity. A blank canvas. It is not long when the Umbrella Friend has my Brother's Wife and her Son sitting translating the song 'Ti-Ti' into Chinese. And then, using specially chosen black pens, they are writing on the canvas, transforming it into a piece of art. Chinese script and hand-drawn flowers and trailing leaves, all in a non-bleeding black ink that sits naturally on the soft off-white. It's as if a spell was cast and, carried on the wind, was captured by a dream-catcher canvas. Poetic art. It is truly magical looking.

In the corner three others are busy crafting crumpet-sized smiley faces from card, having downloaded a selection of cartoon illustrated winking, smiling, laughing emoticons and printed them on coloured paper. The threesome now cut and trim them, attaching short pieces of ribbon for hanging. Dozens already sit in a small breadbasket, beside it a jar of safety pins. Demonstrating how it would work, my Writer Friend brings me over to the coffin where there is a sample of the beaming little faces pinned to the muslin frill that skirts the casket. Flipping one over, I spy a personal message written to my Brother, and I am moved.

The overall effect is better than I imagined. I suspect it is even better than he wished for. Inside, I feel a warm glow shrinking my cloud. I reach for my Writer Friend, embracing her. Bittersweet soft tears of gratitude flow. And she cries gently with me.

TiTi

她准备好了飞翔
穿越天空中的云彩
遥望前方的暴风雨
不管风吹向何方
她也要踏上回家的漫长之路

如果你看见我在斜视
那只是因为我像一块石头一样冷和寂寞
我们找到了一扇黄金的大门
但是我们却丢失了钥匙
在我们入睡之前，让我们一起寻找它
宝贝，求你了

唱我的甜美的情歌
不是平庸的
我们处在终端速度

I flit from one house to the other not wanting to miss a beat. I feel something different. Trepidation? Excitement? I am allowing it in. I find myself beaming with inappropriateness. I love the anticipation of pure devilment over the whole staged Wake setting.

The crowds are beginning to arrive and there is an air of positive energy about the place. My Mother's house is the hospitality hub. Meet and greet, food, refreshments. My Brother's house a hive of traffic and loitering. Unsuspecting mourners make their way into my Brother's house and I watch out for them. Observe them. They stall in the hallway to sign the book of condolences and then again in the main room as if mentally preparing themselves before stepping into the conservatory. To see my dead Brother for the first time. I think they must perceive me as gone mad as I can barely contain my smiling, knowing what they do not. Preparing them, I say, 'Wait till you see' and grabbing a hand I lead them into the conservatory. Those that have settled hover to see the reaction of the new arrivals.

At first their eyes fall on my Brother in the casket. There is a gulp, that flicker of despair, the reality dawning that he really is gone. In the next moment their eyes scan the general scene and down the length of the coffin, and I can feel their emotions shift. A curiosity, what is this they spy? Their brain taking in his look, the umbrella with the Chinese writing, and the mix of flowers strewn all over the casket – the air perfumed sweetly, like a spring that has sprung earlier than expected and is accumulating here. There is no smell of death or decay. No gloom. No Irish wailing. Perhaps they think it is a Chinese tradition. Then they see the smiley faces. At this point I am almost jigging on the spot with anticipation of the pièce de résistance. Some caress the casket frills, others take a smiley face and turn it in their hand cooing at the message. I am short of hurrying them along. And then they turn around the end – the boots. The degrees of reaction vary, but ultimately are all the same. There is another gulp, this time of an alternative emotion. Mirth, laughter, guffaw or glee. They all love it. Hands are clapped, thighs slapped, faces grasped. Their tears are no more. And in that moment they are untroubled. Lifted. Delighted even.

My Brother's wish is granted.

The knowing onlookers join in and the room is filled with shouts of laughter and jubilance. Sharing in the joke. Over and over again.

Our Documentary Friend is there looking on, and I call over to him: 'Mick, get your camera.'

'Oh, I dunno, Lyd. Is it not a bit...inappropriate?'

'No,' I say, making my way over towards him. 'You have to capture this. Ferg wanted people to laugh, not cry, and here it is. You have to record this.' I laugh. 'Sure otherwise no one would believe us.'

He smiles at me. I am right. And he knows it. He leaves the room and returns with his hand-held camera and is soon waltzing around my Brother, around the ballooning crowd. He subtly records and captures reactions as they come in and get to the boots.

My role becomes curator, host. Within a short time I am practised, welcoming people in and escorting them into my Brother. Now I pause a moment to allow them time for seeing the dead and then explain the story behind the umbrella, the smiley faces, his naggin of whiskey tucked into the corner, the ready-poured glass with the straw. All the while slowly bringing them down the side of the casket, baiting them for that moment. With a glint in my eye. And every time, every single time, it ends with laughter. And for that, in those precious moments, I am happy.

As the day shortens, the room fills. The Wake had been reserved strictly for family and close friends. My Mother is overwhelmed with the turnout. And then again, why would she be so surprised? My Brother touched so many hearts. He gave so easily. Anyone that was in his life, even if briefly, was made to feel special. They all felt close to him. He spoke to everyone as if they were the only one in the room. As a result, all and sundry felt they had the right to be at the Wake. Journeyed from near and far.

I am most moved by those that have come to support me in my own grief. The first to arrive, the furthest, has travelled from New York. Abandoning her high-powered job, her husband and kids, to be beside her old boarding school pal in a moment of need. It was a logistical nightmare, but she got here literally by train, plane and automobile. That final leg she managed in the good old Irish way of bumming a lift from Dublin. By virtue of the wonder of social media between text, email and iPhone, she co-ordinated a lift for both my American Cousin and herself with my In-Laws who were travelling down from the capital. We joked about the penance of the journey, but she would be in the good company of my straight-talking Yankee cousin.

And here she is walking across my Brother's room towards me, arms outstretched, and I tear up because my Boarding School Buddy is here and her reasons are not just for respect for my Brother but for her love of me and our history. A new link is soldered in our friendship chain.

I am squeezing her now and we are both crying and rocking where we stand as she holds me tight. It is an energising moment, and I find the bliss of friendship and appreciation exceeds the sadness. Separating, we both laugh and each of us pat under our eyes, a fool's errand at saving our makeup. I take her hand and draw her into the conservatory to my Brother and bring her on the loopy loop of laughter.

The sea of faces is a familiar one. Their tenders tethered to my Brother, the buoy. It is a Wake in more than the traditional sense. It has all the colourful tones of a festival of the dead.

Scanning the crowd, I meet and greet and chat with friends and relatives of old. And they in turn catch up with friends and relatives of old. It is a spinning circle where old connections make new and discover that my Brother had more than touched the lives of so many.

It is the ultimate Green Room as musicians and band-mates gather. As day turns to night instruments are picked up and a jam session the likes of which you would never behold is beheld before us.

My Oldest Pal arrives from Luxembourg with his bemused husband and another link is soldered to my chain. Introductions are made to my writer friends, and squeals of recognition reveal that it is he who is behind one of my book's fictional characters. He chuckles that his reputation has preceded him.

And then my Oldest Girlfriend arrives with her Young Husband and sister in tow, the husband fairly new to the circle. At this stage the party is in full swing. My Sister-in-Law holds my Brother's hand and taps her feet, looking so happy as the musicians belt out and the crowd squeezes in. We are all now facing the corner in the south-west with the piano and fiddle, bodhrán and drum, tin whistle and bass, cello and violin, as song and rhythm carry us all to the heavens.

My Oldest Girlfriend's Husband looks a little shell-shocked at the throng and happenings. I turn to my Oldest Girlfriend, calling above the noise, 'Is he alright?'

My Oldest Girlfriend laughs and leans into me, 'He is a bit awestruck,' she explains and replays their conversation into my ear.

'He said to me, "Cath, that is Glen Hansard." "I know," says I. "And that is Liam O'Maonlaí," he says, nodding at the other fella. "Yes," says I. "And isn't that yur wan from Pulp Fiction?" says he. "Yes," says

I. And pointing over the other side, I say, "and that one there is your one from The Commitments."'

I am laughing because it is indeed a talented mix of all sorts. And I am beaming again. Because that is typical of my Brother. Many found him at different stages of his life. He impressed them all. A real Liquorice All Sorts. He had something for everyone. And now here they all are in the one room to send him off in the way that he knew and loved best. Still striking a chord, making new friends.

The whole time, our Documentary Friend is stood up on the window ledge in the corner capturing the private concert and we are all in the mosh pit and my Brother is rocking in his casket, boots and all. My Sister beckons me and I come on command.

'He's melting,' she says. I look down at my Brother's face and see the waxy sheen of the make-up and worry at the slipping of it. There is a blue-green tinge appearing along his chin line. Death is present again. Without a word I retreat to my Mother's house and to my Father's den. Taking the electric fan I scurry back to the Wake, carrying the fan through the swaying crowd and hand it to my Sister. 'One sec,' I say and I retrieve a high stool from the kitchen. Finding a nearby extension lead, a cord is deftly run under people's feet and the casket and soon we have the fan set up on the high stool blowing cool air on my Brother. All is well again.

My Sister-in-Law watching the setup, not relinquishing her hold on my Brother, nods approval. 'Good, good,' she says and pats my Brother's face affectionately and then turns back towards the musicians.

The room is a squash and a squeeze and in one corner there is the music and the musicians all vying for space to contribute, to be part of the one consciousness that pulses on behalf of my Brother. The rest of the room is feeding off these virtuosi that nourish our souls and grieve theirs. The bottleneck that is the double door to the conservatory drip feeds in and out those that are late arriving and want to pay their respects. I scan the heaving mass, seeking eye contact with those close to my heart, and spy the coffin lid that is propped up on its side under my Brother's work desk.

It stops me.

The world falls away from me.

Music is muted and the crowd stills in my mind's eye.

There is the wrenching reality of it. The small brass plate, the give-away that my Brother's life is finite. Stating his name, birth date and death date. It is a jolt to my being.

'Shit, we have to put the lid on him tomorrow,' I say to no one. The Secret comes to mind again. And I play the mock memory in my head of how he really died, and it is devastating.

We needn't be here at all.

The dam breaks and big fat round tears flow down my cheeks. Conscious of my grief among the joyous, I drop my chin and take up the rhythm of the swaying crowd to try and hide my blubbering heaving short frame in the mass. Unable to help myself, I reach into my Brother and cup his head, stroke his hair, the tears still flowing. And yet would I change it? Would I have him back? Give him his shitty struggling life as it had become?

Feeling a hand go around my shoulder, I turn to look up into the face of my First Cousin. Her timing is perfect and exactly what I need. Without a word, I lean into her embrace, the two of us swaying in rhythm to the crowd. Putting my hand around her waist I squeeze back, allowing the tears to flow. No words are needed. Nothing needs to be said.

Scanning the crowd again, I catch the eye of those not saying the same, and there it is. The unsaid. The glory. The sadness. The bittersweet tremendous send-off that we are giving my Brother and I know it. They know it. The whole room knows it. We are one with him and there is no other place I would rather be than here. Perfection. I am so proud of him, his circle, what he achieved, the gathering a true reflection of the life he lived. I am privileged to have been part of it. Proud to have shared in this life, his crazy life. His crazy wonderful magical musical heaving disabled life.

SATURDAY

February 6

In the morning we discuss the Wake for the success that it was. Like a fantastic house party that had gone off without a hitch. My American Cousin's eyes are bloodshot. From grieving, I am thinking, or the late night or the drink. Probably all three.

'What time did ye finish up?' I ask her, laughing as she plonks two Solpadeine tablets into a glass of water.

'Early,' she says, laughing back. 'Roz got a lift into town with Maurice,' she adds, anticipating my next question.

My Husband strolls into the kitchen and on catching the end of the conversation produces his phone.

'She ended up with Liam and Maurice playing for her,' he chuckles.

'Seriously?'

My Husband is leaning over the breakfast table and pulling up video footage on his screen.

'You videoed it?' I say pleasantly surprised. My Husband turning up trumps again.

'She didn't want to leave on a low note,' he explains, 'so asked Liam to jazz it up some. He took up on the piano and then Maurice joined him in duet, the two of them jamming for her.'

I look, my American Cousin peering over my shoulder, and we watch a closeup of the two pianists play impromptu, finding a natural rhythm, banging out a wonderful jazz piece. My Boarding School Buddy is beaming with joy, tapping out her foot to the sheer wonder of it. My Husband pans the scene with his iPhone, capturing the final send-off with my Brother as key witness to it all.

'Oh, my God, that is fantastic.' I gleefully look up at him. I turn to watch again as the two maestros swap places barely taking their hands off the keys. True skill.

'It is, isn't it?' he says, delighted with himself.

'Roz will love that,' I say. 'Her mom will love it.' And then add, 'You'll have to send her a copy.'

'I will,' he says, 'as soon as I figure out how to upload the video. It is a big file.'

I am still smiling, picturing the intimate crowd that remained hours before dawn. And how special that moment must have been. Including for my Brother.

That time of the night had become his most feared. Dreading sleep. When he would have experienced horrible dreams, only to awake to his new living nightmare. That darkest hour. I have woken then too. Not too often, but enough to understand that feeling of being alone and lost, even if someone is in the bed next to you. Where darkness sits in your belly, your head swamped with no hope. But I always had the choice to get out of bed, turn on a light, make a cup of herbal tea. I reached out to my Brother once at that black hour, in the lowest of lows. And he talked me out of any sinister thoughts, out of the Fear. Fear. My Brother no longer feared death. He had got to a stage where he feared living.

For him on this final night, to have been surrounded by friends and then it trickle down to the few, for the darkest hour to pass with the dawn about to rise over his head in the east, with this motley lot playing out on one final piece. I like to think it would have helped him rest easy to have that last duet at dawn. For that I take great solace.

Dark Days

I've lived through Dark Days
When I couldn't believe.
I've heard every kind word
As a trick to deceive.
Trying to find a voice to wish
But it ending up with a shout.
If you're the one who tells the lie
You're the first to find out.
Oh luck is hard to take
'Cause it takes you by surprise
And when it brings love in its arms
It's harder to be wise.
I fought against it tooth and nail
I've tried to kill it in the womb
And when my last weapon was broke
You took me to your room.
So I'm drinkin' and smokin'
I'm taking pills when I'm not ill
I've enjoyed the most of it
And the truth is I do still
But there's nothing I'd do differently
There's no way I'd change my life
To get a decent cutting edge
Well, you've got to whet the knife.

Today is the day we put a lid on my Brother. The day we would have him leave the house for the last time. Say goodbye to his blue eyes, his gringo moustache, to his chubby nail- bitten-when-lying-in-bed fingers, to his big round belly.

And the reality of that I had yet to process. I couldn't see it for the stratocumulus darkening in my chest. I will put it off.

I need a change of underwear. Packing on the hoof on Tuesday, I had brought the bare minimum with me when a laundry turn-around was the last thing on my mind. Our cat also needs feeding. The escape will do me good.

I make the general announcement in the breakfast room that I need to go home for a few bits, asking my daughters do they need anything. A list of basics is provided.

My Brother's Friend who had travelled from Saudi has been in touch to say that he is crippled with pain following a massive back cramp. I explain to those in earshot that I am expecting him and will bring him to Ballydehob to a chiropractor friend there.

'What time is he coming at?' my Mother asks.

'Around 11:30.'

'Oh good. Ferg will be gone by then.'

The statement of fact jolts me.

'What do you mean?'

'The undertakers are coming at 10 to move him.'

My gut clenches. I check the time on my iPhone. It is nearly that already. Pushing back my chair, I bolt for my Brother's house.

It is too soon. The inevitable is looming. I have no control over the clock. Time is persistent. Relentless. Keeps on moving forward. *Resistance is futile.*

I run across the Bridge of Woe. There is a dampness to the day. The wind blows bitter and drizzle forms a mesh around his house. Stepping in beyond the porch, I pass two Pillars from the undertakers. They are handsomely sombre looking, dressed in matching black coats, standing to attention, with their highly polished shoes. Nodding a quick greeting, I slip into the conservatory where my Brother is lain.

The wicker has been stripped bare, the smiling faces gone, his boots removed, the umbrella placed elsewhere. I panic. They started without me. I feel excluded. Left out. Insignificant.

'Where are all the smiley faces? I ask, subduing my panic.

'We put them in with him,' my Sister explains.

My Sister-in-Law stands by her husband, his limp hand held gently between her two. She is chatting with my Sister's Husband and animatedly gestures with her hands still holding my Brother's. They are a hand-dancing duo. Clearly rigor mortis has not affected my Brother's useless muscles.

My daughters arrive. We are all there now, save my Mother. This is expected. She is consistent in her view and her wish to remember the living as they lived and not to have a final memory of putting a lid on them.

Some of us are busy around my Brother, compelled to add something in with him. I seek a blank smiley face as I had yet to write a personal message myself.

'They were all used,' my Sister explains. I am disappointed. Not wanting to write a note on a mere scrap of paper, I search my mind for an alternative. From one creative person to another, I cannot let my Brother down by shoving something insignificant into his casket. And then it comes to me.

I go where I know he has kept spare copies for gifting to unsuspecting visitors and take out a paperback of my teen novel, *K-Girls*. My Brother, my critic, my backer, had funded the loan to enable me to self-publish my teen book, and now I could write a personal note to him in one and include it with him. Some light reading for his onward journey. It would be placed in amongst the smiley faces, his tobacco pouch, his wee dram of whiskey, a tomato ketchup sachet (he loved his take-aways).

In the end they would all turn out the same, a pile of ash, but there is an importance in the act of including a token that means something to each of us. Meant something to me more than it could now to him.

My Sister-in-Law holds his hands still and then says something in Chinese to her son. He turns to me and says she wants to rub his feet. I know I am frowning when I look to her.

'You know, Ferr always like his feet rub – you think I rub his feet?' she asks, pleadingly.

Anything is possible with this formidable woman. Not knowing what to expect, I attempt to lift the linen that covers my Brother's lower half and realise it is stuck down along the edge of the casket. Hesitating, I lean down and spy in through a gap towards my Brother's feet. I am relieved to see he is lain out as requested in his paisley PJs and wearing his thick speckled wool socks. His legs intact. I had imagined a macabre scene of broken, or worse still, severed limbs. The mortician's solution to straighten my Brother's contracted muscles in the casket.

'Yes, Li.'

I examine the stitching at the edge and see that the linen frill has been stapled, not sewn. I prise at the little piece of metal but don't have the manual strength to pull up the silver teeth without tearing the cloth.

'Have you got a scissors?' I ask my Step-Nephew and he retrieves some from my Brother's desk nearby. I log how easily he found them and register that this too was his home. He arrived as a teenager and left as a man. My Brother becoming his father, in kind if not in name. My Step-Nephew's face has aged in the past twenty-four hours. How right is the old saying *'Grief is the price we pay for love'*. I smile gently at him and work around the end of the casket to free enough of the material to allow a hand in.

'Try now, Li,' I say.

She steps around me and slips her hand blindly inside.

'Ai-Ya!' she exclaims, and I jump with fright.

'He still have socks on,' she says, laughing.

'Yes,' I say, forgetting that my Brother's Wife had had no idea what clothes were selected for him.

'You think I take socks off?' She is asking for permission.

I visualise my Brother's feet and not knowing the science, I inwardly freak out at the thought of her rubbing his flesh only for it to slide away in her hands.

I look to her son, 'Probably better not, the flesh…we don't know…'

My Step-Nephew says something in Chinese and my Sister-in-Law laughs out loud. I smile at her. My Brother would be laughing with her. Their black morbid humour was matched. It is one of the reasons he loved her.

Her hands work away under the cover. 'Ferr always like my massage. Help him *relaaax.*'

She draws out the word relax, and I feel my own shoulders release. She is telling the room. 'He love his feet massage" And she smiles away content in her role of wife and masseuse as we all look on in appreciation and bewilderment.

One of the Pillars approaches the door silently. It is a nudge that it is time. My Sister-in-Law moves back up to the position of holding my Brother's hand and we are all silent. We stand around, no one knowing the protocol. Each gravitates towards their loved ones. I to my Husband, my Son to me, my two teen daughters to each other. My Sister leans against her husband, my niece and nephew and Step-Nephew close by. My Father stands alone by my Brother's piano.

On a chair, my Brother's school friend, the Poet, sits. My Brother's best friend and, for a short time during young love's years, his betrayer – and now he sits quietly to pay homage, and it is okay. He is meant to be here. Unobtrusive, quiet, still, bringing his Buddhist Zen to the room.

My Sister-in-Law starts to talk. To no one in particular. To us all.

'You know when I first come to Irulun I am stranger here. This not my home. This mamma home.'

I look to my Sister, glance at my Father, fearing what is to come.

'For first months Mamma cook and share. Sometime I cook for myself: noodle, dim sum.' My Sister-in-Law laughs. 'Then one day, Ferr' ask me to cook a little dinner for him. He say, "Li, tonight you cook me little dinner?" I *sooo* excited.' She stamps her foot to reflect this. We all smile. My Sister-in-Law sways from one foot to the other, still holding my Brother's hand. Using it to conduct while she shares her story.

'I go to shop. Buy many thing. This dinner special. Must make *evvvverybody* like my dinner.' She is laughing. 'Mamma and Papa come to house to eat.' We all look to my Father, and he is smiling and nodding, enjoying the memory.

'Everybody eat,' she continues, grinning from ear to ear. 'Ferr so happy. I happy. All food eat.' We are all smiling at her. I feel a lump rise in the back of my throat.

'Family so important,' she says gesturing to us all in the circle with my Brother's hand. 'So much love – good family. Ferr' love so much. Mama, Pappa, Sisters, Brothers,' she looks to my Sister and our Husbands.

I am in floods. Big fat tears are flowing down my cheeks.

'Children good, much respect.'

I glance around the room and see my Father has taken out his iPhone and is recording her. It feels natural. As it should be captured. This moment of sharing. I realise then that in the twenty or so years that my Sister-in-Law has lived among us, I never have heard, no, listened, to her side of the story. She has always been under the shadow of my Brother. He would speak for her. Make decisions for her. If we wanted to ask something of her, to babysit, to pick up the children from school, to come for dinner. It was always communicated through my Brother. Here she is now talking like I never heard before, sharing with us. My Brother's Wife talks and talks, sharing the story of how they first met, her view. Not ours nor his. From her perspective. And it is fresh, full of colour, and love and happiness.

It is a privilege to witness her outpour. I feel humbled. My Sister-in-Law's face is animated, joyful as she feeds off the memories. Her memories. Her memories shared with my Brother. And that is when I realise that I had not known it. Or at least never been witness to it. Her love for him. Up until this moment, her love for him was private.

When it came to family, my Brother had no choice. He was stuck with us, tied by blood and years of dedication and waiting. There is no denying the love. That was always there. We were an integral part of a family nucleus.

My Brother's freedom of choice extended to his friends, whose company he would select as worthy of his time. For it was precious. And then there was his choice of whom to love. My Sister-in-Law. Here she is radiating in it. There is an aura of white brightness flowing from her to him and, as mad as it may sound, he to her. My Brother may be dead, but there is no denying the love that still binds them.

'One day I in Cyprus,' my Sister-in-Law goes on, 'know no one. No English. Ferr' in hospital. I give him massage. He like massage. I give acupuncture. He no like acupuncture. No like needles.'

Some of us laugh through our tears. We all know how my Brother despised needles.

'Every day I come, ask, "Pain"?' He get dictionary. I know nowhere. English-Chinese. He find word for sick. 病 Bíng. Needle make him sick. After, I just do massage.' She looks to us all smiling. 'He kind. He talk to me. I no English. Every day he teach me. Make me laugh.'

We know this story. But not from this angle. It was always told by my Brother. How he fell for her while recovering from the brink of death from pneumonia picked up while holidaying with us in Cyprus. His fear of needles. How he had tried to put up with them for the first couple of tries but in the end he had to somehow tell her to stop. His sourcing of a dictionary, his need to talk to her, keep her in his company, despite her busyness. Every day she would come and every day he would teach her a few more words. He would use his doodle pens to write the words. Every day she would leave with a pen. Eventually he was healthy enough to get out of bed. Draw again. He had no pens. She had them all. He found his way down to the kitchens where the indentured Chinese worked off their contract. His timing was off. Peak lunch time and she was too busy to come out to him.

Later, she came up after lunch and stormed into his room screaming angrily at him: 'Peh, you want peh.' Firing the pens at him. 'Here your peh.' Thus sealing fate and my Brother's knowledge that he was going to marry this crazy, wonderful woman.

There is a moment when I feel it is time. Squeezing my Husband's hand, I step towards my Brother, lean in and kiss his forehead one last time. It is cold to the touch; waxy, clammy. I tell myself he is no longer here, and yet I cannot process that logic. I pat his hair, his cheek and turn away, forcing one step, then another. I don't look back. Leaving the room, I pass the two Pillars who nod respectfully.

How many have they witnessed do the same? How many have

walked past them over time? Many with tears, with sadness, with anger, perhaps some with joy? The tales they could tell.

Leaving my Brother's house, I pause on the Bridge of Woe. Over there is my Mother's house, behind me my Brother's. The day is clouded and cold and dirty. All the colour sucked out of it. I take stock. Mindful of the here and now. My family in his, my Mother in hers, and I stood somewhere in-between, wondering where the spirit of my Brother has gone. The science of it. For as matter we cannot just cease to be. I firmly believe that. I am not religious enough or scientific enough to have a clear view on it other than his energy has had to go somewhere. Looking skyward I am hoping for a sign. For the clouds to part, or a bird to land on a nearby branch. Perhaps a clap of thunder. But there is nothing. Perhaps his attention is elsewhere; perhaps in the room with his Wife as he should be. No doubt blushing at her gushing, beaming with pride, *morto* at the lot of us streaming with tears.

'They are moving him,' my Husband announces gently and I move from my Mother's kitchen and make my way out to witness my Brother's last journey from his house. There is a small gathering of family at his front door, and there is the hearse that will carry him away. He is already pushed into place, his casket having been carried by whomever, and I am just in time to witness the hearse door being closed on him. The two Pillars walk around to the front. My eye is drawn towards a movement down the drive. It is my Brother's Friend, the one who travelled from Saudi. He is on time to be brought to the chiropractor. And to see his friend's send off. It is poignant timing as the hearse moves off slowly down the drive and the two friends pass each other. It is a moment that I suppose my Brother's Friend will cherish.

Some follow to the church to help with the final arrangements there.

My Husband to help co-ordinate it. I choose not to go. Liberated from responsibility, grief affording me the license not to have to volunteer or commit where I am not willing or able. I feel as if my part in the celebration is complete. I have managed to pull off his Wake as per my Brother's wishes. Boots, smiley faces, and one hell of a party.

There is more to come. For now, I want to seek solace in my Mother's house, pour myself a drink. Then I remember I must feed the cat. And bring my Brother's Friend to have his bones repositioned.

Life continues. In spite of us.

All is quiet at Little House. The cat comes out from the forest hurrying towards me, calling out as he runs. It warms my heart. Scooping him up, I nuzzle his neck and rub my cheek to his, all the time talking and cooing to him. His body buzzes from purring and he responds to my cat hugs by repeatedly nudging my cheek. With the cat in hand, I push into my house and the waft of neglected domesticity greets me. Dirty laundry, unemptied bins, rancid fruit. Nothing too offensive, but the housewife in me registers it and immediately I dismiss it again. This too shall wait. I will have all the time in the world to deal with it. For now it is to focus on feeding the cat and grabbing the few bits that are needed. I try to recall what I was doing this time last week. What I would be doing next? It will be a new normal in any case. Moving on. I think about a few weeks back when both my Brother and his Music Friend were still alive. The difference of time and circumstances. Both lives ended too soon. Too early. What could happen in the next two weeks, and the next after that?

All the necessary done at Little House, I return to Ballydehob village to pick up my Brother's Friend. He is done with the back clicking and appears more comfortable now that my Chiropractor Friend has worked his magic – that and the two tablets someone slipped him earlier. With his bloodshot eyes and lolloping gait, he lowers himself into the car seat and we head west back towards death. 'So, how are you doing?' I ask him.

'Oh, I'm all right.'

I'm not sure if he is referring to his back or in general.

'Jesus, Lydia, I can't believe he's dead.'

'I know. It's all a bit surreal.'

My car's engine is not healthy and threatens to stall. We jerk along a bit, I pumping gas and squeezing the steering wheel tighter as if that will help.

'Sorry about this shitty car,' I laugh.

'I'm glad for the lift,' he says.

The car jerks again, and then as if it has caught its breath, settles once more. 'The last thing I need is a breakdown today,' I joke.

'What time is the funeral?' he asks.

'Three-ish; we are due at 2.30, you know, for the meet and greet,' I say. 'But I don't think it will really get going till five.' It sounds like a party instead of a funeral.

He looks at his watch, 'It's one now. Suppose there is time for lunch somewhere.'

'Yeah,' I hold my tongue at offering lunch at ours, or rather my Mother's. Despite the mountain of donated food, I know too well that my Mother is not receptive to visitors.

'How is Hannah?' I ask about his daughter, changing the subject.

'She is good. It was her who rang me. Jesus, I was in bits, Lydia. Work wasn't so understanding but I didn't give a shit. I had to come.'

'I know,' I say quietly.

'That's what did my back in, I think. The stress of it, and twenty-eight hours of flights. I'm wrecked.'

'Yeah,' I acknowledge. And my Brother is dead.

'Thanks for arranging this.'

'No bother.'

'Yeah, Li wasn't able to fit me in.'

I nearly swallow my tongue. 'Jesus, you asked Li?'

In my head I am thinking what sort of a person asks his widowed friend to fix his back, give him a massage on the day of her Husband's funeral? And then I realise that at least he is being consistent. He can't help himself. He has always been self-focused. Despite his misgivings, there is no denying his loyalty or the grief he is experiencing. He is carrying a sadness that pools in every crease, his own shadow cloud clinging to him.

We come round the bend that marks the start to Schull and the turn off for my Mother's house.

'Will I drop you into the village?'

'Yeah, that would be great.'

I drive up to the front of the village hotel and he gets out using the grab handle of the passenger door to swing himself out.

'You'll have some fun later after a few scoops. I think you should be on for a good night.' I say, trying to inject some lightness.

'Yeah,' he says. Smiling sadly, he shuts the door.

I lean down to wave at the back of him but he has already moved on, swallowed up by his own grieving mist.

I am missing my Husband. A part of me resents that his attention and focus is on helping with the arrangements of the funeral. I have to remind myself that he is doing what he needs to do. He is doing what he does best.

A natural hotelier, he works well under pressure. The added advantage of being a procrastinator results in performing brilliantly to a short deadline. Troubleshooting last-minute issues and snags at conferences and music festivals after months of organising. And here he is helping to co-ordinate the funeral, which involves speeches, readings, music and set up. A sensitive dance around the many professionals, some with egos that no doubt will result in a highly talent-full gig. At three days' notice.

I would have him by my side, but to what end? My own comfort, yes, but against his own. He would be like a child told to sit still in the classroom when the sun is shining and the clock ticks the last agonising minutes till home time. Foot jigging under the desk with a hankering to be elsewhere.

I may be surrounded by people and loved ones but I am still lonely. I feel a need to go off and have coffee with him alone. I would go off and drink a bottle of wine with him. Two. One each perhaps. Or walk a long mile with him and the dogs. Who am I kidding? I can barely manage the walk from one house to the other. The walk and I can wait. Not so sure about the wine.

My Mother's house is quiet. People are in their own rooms getting ready for the funeral.

I will wear full black. My wardrobe is full of it. And there are outfits that come straight to mind, take little effort, usually with good end results. I had grabbed an old reliable when at Little House feeding the cat. Now I stand in my Mother's and take in how I look. I want to look smart but not fashioned. Vanity is the devil for company when you know you are not supposed to be the centre of attention. Yet my Brother knows me well enough to understand that I will still make an effort. Simple black fitted knee-length dress with leopard-print belt, black tailored jacket, flesh stockings, leopard-print heels. My hair carries some of the coiffed-look still. I wear it loose around my shoulders. Blunt fringe.

I am not happy with my face. I have aged the last few days. Lines have formed around my eyes and purple shadows hug puffy bags that cling there too. I look pasty. Even my freckles have a green tinge to them.

A sore has risen on my cheek. It is bigger than a spot and has festered. A scab has formed, and it weeps a little. I know it is infected. The punishment of vanity. Or perhaps as a result of carrying the Secret. Like in Dorian's Grey portrait, where the badness seeps onto the canvas.

I surmise the truth. A pin prick from my beauty treatment was kissed too often in the last few days and I picked up something from someone else's lips. A poisoned kiss. I am guessing a herpes virus snuck in and settled there. I do not have time to get to a doctor or chemist. I attempt to cover it with concealer, but that only congeals there, clinging to the rise and bumps on the smarty-sized oozing sore.

Giving up, I follow through with my foundation, blusher. It will not be a good day for eye make-up but I apply my *cat's eye* flicks anyway, and lots of water-proof mascara. It is all part of the look. I don't bother with my usual red lipstick. Thinking that is probably pushing vanity too far.

Dressed and face on, there are minutes to spare.

My Mother is sat at her desk with her coffee and fag. She is dressed in purple and lilac. Like in the Bible. Like the priests. Like me on my wedding day. No black for her. Even her shoes and jewellery match. Purple. And all the global interpretations that go with it. Mourning. Courage. Sacred. Position. Fasting. Faith. Patience. Trust. Reconciliation. What is to come.

'Where is everyone?' I ask.

'I have no idea,' she says, calmly, 'presumably getting ready.' She sucks on the cigarette and blows smoke. 'Did you try Li's?'

I note how my Mother has switched occupancy.

'No,' I say, and without another word head on down. The lower house is buzzing. The conservatory is full of musicians practising. A full circle of celebrities, my Brother's friends, and it reminds of the days of old in Dublin when as a college student I would turn up at my Brother's gaff that was the old Winstanley shoe factory, and there would be a session taking place. Grunge heads sitting in a circle, squinting at each other through the hash fog, plucking away at their instruments.

Only now the main element was missing. The nucleus – my Brother. And then I see my Brother's boots. Someone has placed them smack centre, and the musicians are all focused on these. Trance-like. There is a small crowd hovering, looking on, and there in the midst of them my Sister and Sister-in-Law. I catch my Sister's eye.

'It's nearly three,' I call over. My Sister nods at me.

'Li,' she calls over. 'We must go now.'

'Go now?' my Sister-in-Law is surprised. 'Funeral at five.'

Damn it. Lost in the detail again.

'Yes, Li, the funeral is at five,' my Sister explains, 'but the family tradition of shaking hands and meeting people is at three.'

'Ai-ya!' my Sister-in-Law stamps her foot. 'Musicians come now?'

'No, Li. They come later.'

'Ok, I wait,' she says, satisfied.

'No, Li,' my Sister forces. 'You wife. You most important person. Must come now.' My Sister has resorted to broken banter again.

I nod at my Sister-in-Law to show that I am in agreement with my Sister.

The front door opens and my Eldest comes in. She is dressed in black trousers and an off-the-shoulder crop-top. The mother in me immediately judges it is inappropriate for both the funeral and the weather.

'Have you no jacket?' I ask, sternly.

'No, Mom,' she frowns impatiently, 'that's why I came down'. She turns to her Aunt. 'Li, do you have a jacket I could borrow?'

'Jacket – yes, one moment.' And her Aunt scurries into my Brother's bedroom. Seconds later she is out with his tux jacket and my Daughter dons it with pride. It transforms her. A perfect fit, save the slightly long sleeves. She instantly rolls them up, revealing the burgundy silk lining that co-incidentally matches the flower pattern on her Bardot top. It is an up-styled vintage 80's look. We all smile. It is perfect.

'You keep,' my Sister-in-Law announces. 'Ferr' would want you to keep.'

I believe she is right. The jacket would not fit any of the rest of us. Certainly not my Sister-in-Law with her tiny Chinese frame. The five-foot-ten frame of my Eldest carries it beautifully. My Daughter straightens, as if standing to attention, jutting her chest, raising her chin, grinning.

'Thanks, Li.' She steps in for a hug, almost dwarfing her Aunt.

My Sister-in-Law pats my Daughter's shoulder awkwardly, giggling with satisfaction.

I can't help but imagine how it might have looked on my Brother had he stood up long enough, been a healthy big Brother. I can feel my cloud loom again.

I look at my phone: 'We need to go.'

Making my way out of my Brother's, I turn my back on the musicians and the music. Out on the drive I realise that I have no transport. My Husband is already at the church. I glance around at the parked cars, not recognising many and turn to my Sister, who is trailing behind me.

'I'll have to get a lift with someone.'

'Where is Jackson?' my Sister asks. 'Is he gone already?'

I have no idea where my youngest is. Hours have gone by since I have seen him. Did I even see him today? Oh, yes, he was at the closing of the coffin.

'He's watching telly,' my Daughter announces. Of course he is. What was it he had said earlier? 'Best week ever – Uncle Ferg gets to walk again in heaven. And I get a whole week off school.'

Habit has led me to the side entrance of the church.

It is as if it is Christmas Day. The church is thronged, benches sagging with the weight of the community. I let the door swing quietly behind me and step into the mix. The altar is speckled with candles and storm lanterns of all shapes and sizes. The space is silent. Scanning the open areas, my Husband is nowhere to be seen and I am at a loss as to where I am supposed to sit. Front pew I know, but which side? My eyes roll over the crowd. All their eyes on me. I am the first of the immediate family to arrive.

So many familiar faces. Friend's faces bring gentle smiles or nods of heads. All these people's spirits lifting me up as if supporting me by the elbow or placing a gentle hand on my shoulder. My heart warms and pulsates a gentle soundwave, dissipating my cloud some. The love in the room is almost tangible. I am walking towards the centre crossing of the church and spying my Writing Friend arriving too. I lean in and take a hug, whispering, 'I don't know where I should sit'.

She scans the front pews like I had done and gestures to the pew nearest to me.

'Sure sit there for now, and I'm sure you'll be grand.'

She looks about the church, looking for someone or something.

'The rest will follow soon,' I say, reassuring myself as much as to say something in return and I let her pass.

Conscious that eyes are on me I bow from the waist briefly, a boarding school learned habit, and glide into the seat. Back straight, knees together, I clasp my hands and only then allow my eyes to rise to the space that I have been avoiding. They rest on my Brother's casket.

Of course it is the reason we are all here, yet the reality hits home and I suck in a big silent breath. Adjust my bottom on the seat. Breathe. Releasing it slowly.

There has been a continuous activity going on that I only now become aware of. As the church continues to fill, the altar and transept are busy with a small team of discreet professionals who are setting up mikes, trailing leads, adjusting camera pods and large speakers as if for a film-set. Silent distraction for the waiting crowd.

My Husband appears out from the Sacristy all business-like and, spying me, glides over to where I am sitting. I am expecting a kiss and get one briskly on the cheek with whispered instructions: 'You need to move over to the other side.' Explaining, 'That's where the family will sit.'

I acquiesce and diligently move, bowing my departure and repeating the movement again on the other side.

My Husband and I got married here in this little church, twenty years before. And the same family and much the same friends were gathered then too. That was still a time when fathers of the bride footed the bill and mothers controlled the invitation list. My Father, ever generous and glad in heart, ensured that all could attend. The family of my Sister's Husband, her friends and the friends of my Brother were all invited too. It was a big wedding.

Even back then we didn't know what life was left for my Brother and so every celebration was exactly that, a celebration. My wedding was no exception. It was a great party. My Brother was in the church that day too, not far from where he lies now. But then he was surrounded by his musician friends, a small group of whom to play as I walked up the aisle with both my Mother and Father on my arm to give me away. My Brother was silent that day too, suffering from death of a different kind: a massive hangover. He had gone too far the night before, drinking with his friends. It was another reunion, he having not seen so many in so long. The morning of my wedding he couldn't brush his teeth with the retching. He was to have sung for me at the church but his hangover was too bad for that. At that time, my Brother could still bring his arms to his face, and with shaking hands played his tin whistle instead. The sound of the accompanying cello, guitar, and fiddle disguising any tremor in his tune. To say I was disappointed would be putting it lightly. But exchanging vows soon masked any upset and with time it became another clip in my memory slideshow.

Here we are again, including many that attended my wedding day, and then some. Today is indeed another celebration albeit for a different reason, but it was becoming obvious to me that while my Brother will not sing on this day either, the gathering was going to be an even more magnificent one.

More and more still come, and at some point so do my Daughters, my Son, my Sister, my Father, my Sister-in-Law and her Son. My mind does not register their arrival and yet here they are, and in that same moment I register that my Mother is not.

'Where's Mom?' I ask my Father who is sat beside me.

'She's on the way.' He shuffles his bottom on the seat, patting his pockets, checking for his bits and bobs. I see his eye rest on my Brother's casket. There is a flicker of pain and he turns away again, head bent. Sliding closer to him, I slip my hand round his lower back and stroke him, trying to rub the suffering away. His cumulus and mine push together. Stacking. Ready for the rain.

I scan the crowd behind me and see the line of people that have begun to form in order to pay their respects. Where is my Mother? The line starts to move slowly and then it has begun. The handshaking. I fear that my Mother has decided to give the church a miss.

My Mother was never one for funerals. It has been some years since she lost her own mother, her only brother before that, and her father before that. Never seeing them laid out, nor visiting their grave. Preferring to keep those lost close to her 'in here', she would say, patting her chest. It was a gesture I did not pay much attention to in earlier years when she spoke about her deceased family. But I have noticed in the last few days and in particular her determination about it. Not a gentle patting with her flat palm as before, but a poke or a jabbing with her own arthritic bent finger. Dab-dabbing like it is given with authority, or pushing something home. Subconsciously telling us and those lost, that they are held there. They are not going anywhere. As if they had a choice in the matter.

I turn in the pew and catch my Aunt's eye. They are old pals. My Aunt, the widow of my late Uncle, my Father's brother. Sisters through marriage, love and loss, life and consequence. Smoking buddies.

'Have you seen Mom?' I mouth to her, turning back to accept the next hand of sympathy, making eye contact and turning back to my Aunt again.

She shakes her head.

Between the last flesh pressing and the next I quickly turn again and gesture to her by putting my hand to my face, thumb to ear, my pinky to lips and mouth, 'Can you call her?'

My Aunt is already reaching for her bag when I turn back again.

Faces make their way along. The gesture varies slightly between the sympathetic nod while gripping the hand and others who utter the universal words, 'I'm sorry for your loss.'

Most make eye contact, few don't. The handgrip varies from the knuckle breaking to the damp and limp. I adjust my rings on my right hand to try and lesson any discomfort.

I usually struggle to remember names. But now, for everyone I know or have met, their name pops into my mind and my mouth speaks it.

It is an anomaly.

I can't explain it. I respect a person and their name, I understand the majority only have the one. Yet I can know it one day and find it has hidden in that empty space in my head the next. I may know a person for years and have called them by name frequently, and yet in a moment my brain draws a blank. It has become a joke among true friends; others still take offence.

Yet here I am, seeing someone approach, my brain processing their face, pulling it up in my head and I see their name form as if typed, in my front eye. Name after name.

I register my Father struggling to recognise those that move along. Leaning in as they advance, I whisper at his shoulder, announcing the next and the next. I only stick on those I have not met before and most have the grace to introduce themselves, explain their connection.

The line is out the door, the church porch, and beyond. We had been sitting and would stand to hug someone close. But as they keep coming, so do the hugs and so I stay standing to meet them. My Father stands beside me. I adjust my stance, putting my weight on one high heel or the other. My right hand is tiring. As I turn to witness the mile, I see my Mother enter and make her way over to us in her lilac. She is a splash of colour merging into the front pew against the greys and blacks worn by the rest of us. My Brother would like that. She slips in beside my Sister and takes up the next hand that comes along, as though she was there all the time, falling into rhythm with the rest of us. As if it came naturally to her.

I notice my Sister-in-Law has moved behind to the second pew. I ask my Father why she is not staying up front.

'Deng Li is on his own. She wants to be next to him.'

Of course. She has moved to be next to her son. My Brother's kin are up front. My Step-Nephew has been alone. With everyone else respecting the rule of reserved pews for the grieving family, no one has sat next to him.

'People are walking past them,' my Mother states, leaning towards us. 'They don't know who they are.'

It is true. Only those that do know my Brother's Wife and Stepson, pay their respects directly. Others pass them both by. There are decades of connections who pass, too many from a time before my Sister-In-Law, those who knew my Brother as the boy and the teen, not the married man. They do not know who she is. Or they are only focused on the front pew.

The trail is a lucky dip of decades of familiar faces. There is my Brother's childhood friend, his ex-girlfriend, his national school buddy, his old teacher, his childhood doctor, another old friend's Mother, his old neighbours, the barman. My friends, parents of friends, my Father's friends, my Father's business buddies, my Sister's friends, her relations through marriage. My in-laws. The outlaws. On and On. Click. Click. Wispy strands of memories resurface. Vignettes. The whole process plays like a slideshow in my head. Each has their specific connection to my Brother's forty-eight years of life. Each one bringing up a flicking snapshot of a special time.

Here are the friends from when we went 'trick or treating' to the village pub, playing the tin-whistle, some of us dancing, others passing the cap. Here are the friends he made a camp with in the forest and I and mine infiltrated it. And here are those friends who put on the garage plays with parents and pets for an audience. And that friend with the chemistry set who nearly blew up the garden shed. Here come the summer and the sailing school friends. The teen's disco friends and village loitering friends. The boarding school friends who camped in at ours for a weekend, ate twenty-four loaves and got through forty litres of milk. The musician friends at his surprise twentieth in the old shoe factory. Here are those from the all night smoked-filled jam sessions, the late-night gig friends. The travelling friends who had a lock-in with moustachioed musicians in some Portuguese síbín. The rescue friend who brought him home drunk having got lost on a Cypriot goats' path. The friend who picked him up whenever he fell over, the put-him-to-bed friend, the ones who would keep him company when he spent hours hung-over and that friend who would bring him his pints of tea or port depending on the humour. The handy friends who could service his wheelchair, mix a set, brew up some magic, deal him his drugs. The professionals who became friends, the printing guy, the picture-framing guy, his Home Help, his community nurse, his physiotherapist, the guy whose burgers he loved, his other doctor, the engineer, the other musician buddies. The other engineer, the sound guy, the ticket guy, the graphics guy, the hoist fitter, the physio, the doctors, the nurses, hospital staff. The expected, the unexpected. Those conspicuous in their absence.

On and on they come, as if playing a slide show. Projecting from his life's carrousel. Click. Click.

The *Oh's* and the *Ah's*, the hugs and embraces. Us comforting them, the next comforting us.

On and on. Click. Click.

His life story a moment held by each person coming to share their respect. I had no grasp of this before. And now it comes to me. Each one as important as the next. A moment of symbiosis. Each one of us is giving as much as taking. Sharing.

Gratitude. That is the feeling that bubbles to the surface within me. The importance of each and every one of us to each other. The butterfly effect. The 'It's a Wonderful Life' effect.

How grateful I am to each and every one of you. Your contribution to his life. His to yours. How you all linked to him and he to you. To each memory bestowed, you captured his essence. As if each and every one of them hold a part of him now within. He lives on in each individual that passes. Their handshake, hugs and embrace the seal of the deal. His story, their story. My story. As one. He will love on in them, in us. In the form of a glow, a spark, a light captured. As if shining from behind a window in their souls. A cloud of souls. Soul clouds. Stacking. Not for rain now but for something else. It is a wonderful feeling. The love that is radiating from within me, from them. All around.

I am humbled. Honoured to bear witness, to receive and to give.

Shake, hug, nod. Click. Click.

'Sorry for your loss.'

'Thank you, thank you.'

'Sorry for your loss.'

'I know, thank you.

'Sorry for your loss.'

'You're so good…'

'Sorry for your loss.'

'Thank you for coming.'

'Sorry for your loss.'

'Yes, yes, thank you.

'Sorry for your loss.'

The musicians appear at the atrium door. Familiar heads fill the ope, glancing out as if waiting for their moment on stage, awaiting their cue. Hands hold guitars, violins, a double base. Hold each other. They filter out quietly and take up different seats where the church choir would normally sit. An orchestra in the making. My Brother's friends. Comrades. Colleagues. Accompaniments. Fellows. Pals. My nervous looking guitar-playing nephew in the midst of the Oscar winner, the world famous, the infamous. All sitting together in the choir. Brothers and sisters in arms.

An eclectic mix.

The congregation is in for a treat. No, a performance of a lifetime.

I can feel it. The kinetic pulse held in suspense. Ready for an electrical storm. A supercell. Rain-band. The crowd know it too. We all shift in our seats.

This is not going to be just a funeral service. This is a celebration. A requiem.

A rhapsodic requiem. A rhapsodic requiem with rocks on.

I witness a verbal walk down memory lane as my Brother's oldest friend takes to the pulpit. He shares his school-day memories of bicycles and chases, a hunger for life and the fearless energy that my Brother possessed. It is followed by his Poet Friend who talks of days in secondary school and a time of wobbly legs, piggy backs, music and the birth of his band *Interference*. His old Dublin House Mate talks of life post school and the college of rock-n-roll life; then it is the Oscar Winner talking about discovery of the Cork wine-drinking musicians' underground at the old Shoe Factory, followed by the Documentary Making Friend who talks of a life *sustained by friendship and love*. My Brother the wheelchair bound, the musician of musicians. In between the stories are the songs. The Gift giving. My Father takes to the pulpit stoically. Waves of pure unfiltered emotion, troughs and peaks that were the journey of his

Son's life. All the while the priest sits and listens and nods and smiles. It is extraordinary.

I know my Brother would have loved it. There are moments even when I forget he is dead and his remains lie horizontally. I expect him to come out from the back any moment now to sing one of his own songs – the main act.

Watching the musicians, they are putting their heart and soul into it. While one sings, others cry. Professional to the core, none of them break while performing themselves, selecting to do so quietly when the spotlight is no longer on them. It is so admirable. Again my Brother would have expected that too. The perfectionist to the end.

And then I am taken aback as my Eldest joins the troupe. It is unexpected. Unannounced. Unaccompanied. She starts to sing a Capella. There is no other sound.

'Of all the money that I e'er had, I spent it in good company.'

My heart leaps in my chest, her voice a sweet swirling eddy that sweeps beneath my skin skimming my nerves pulling them to attention. I spot the Oscar winner do a double take and lean forward cocking his ear to listen more intently. Smiling. She doesn't see him, for her eyes are closed and she is focused inwardly on the song and its meaning.

'And of all the harm that e'er I've done, alas it was to none but me.

And all I've done for want of wit, to memory now I can't recall.

So fill to me the parting glass. Goodnight and joy be with you all.'

Her clear, soft meaningful tones are carried over my head on a wave of regret and goodbyes. The words are so poignant and appropriate for my Brother. The tears flow again down my cheeks and I reach for my already sodden tissues to try and muffle my sobs.

My tears are not just for grief. They are also for relief. Satisfaction even.

My Eldest's last words with my Brother had not been a positive experience. His Oscar Winning Friend had asked while in her company if she could sing too, and my Brother had answered for her: that her voice was 'all right – like a lot of teens nowadays it's a bit x-factorish.'

This was not a compliment, and neither was it taken as one. She had intended to have it out with her Uncle, but left it be when his Music Friend died, and then she had to go back to boarding school, promising herself that she would talk to my Brother over mid-term...

Here now in the church she gets to prove him wrong as the church listens to her. While I could not hold it together, she does throughout, and only at the last lines does her voice quiver. The professional troupe pick up on her hesitation and they and the congregation join in with the final lines to carry her.

'Come fill to me the parting glass, good night and joy be with you all.'

My heart soars with pride for my beautiful girl. She did her Uncle proud and, I suspect, put some things right in her mind too.

I do not want it to end. But it must. And then the Priest is there with his thurible and incense and holy water, and I am reminded once more of the dead and the mortality of us all. A hush engulfs the church as the priest swings the chains and puffs of incense waft around my Brother's casket. This is followed by the blessing with holy water. All the while I watch on and reflect. Inside I am grateful that the priest has elected to say the final prayer silently, having read the congregation and moment perfectly. I take comfort from the familiar smell of frankincense and myrrh that I associate with happier times in my alma mater and recall the melodic chants of the Sisters of Benedict in Connemara. The child in me would escape there now. And yet the Sister that I am would not be anywhere else but here beside my Brother. My Brother lying there in his stocking feet and paisley PJs, lying east to west. East where the sun is yet to rise on another day when he would not. West towards the sunset so often witnessed by those blue blue eyes, closed now forever.

It is done. There is a shift in the congregation as my Husband co-ordinates with a discrete nod and shuffle of those pre-selected. My Eldest, her two cousins, my Husband, Brother-in-Law, and our Archivist Friend get into position to carry my Brother out. Wait, what's that? My Brother's spoken voice breaks across the church speakers and briefly I think he is here and it is all a cruel joke. And then my heart plummets and my head sees reason to register it is a recording followed by his own song 'Sail On'.

The heartache of it.

When the cue is given, the rest of the family fall in behind and pick up the rocking tempo to that of the casket carriers.

There is a pause, the weight is adjusted on the shoulders of the bearers, and after a brief moment we take up the step again. My Brother is being carried by us all. Not just the bearers, but we are all there carrying him within; he is filling the space in my rib cage and gaps around my heart, my stomach and my organs.

We haven't gone far when there is another pause and the bearers flounder. My Brother is too heavy, and after a brief signal, two more instinctively step in to help take the weight. My Husband's Brother and Brother-in-Law step up. They can do nothing about the rest of us who are behind, left to struggle alone.

Sail On

The moon is a ship at night
And it sails over a starry sea.
And its sailors seek out lovers
To hear things they're saying to each other

Well if life was a fairy tale
Every word, would come true.
And as you lie here by my side
I'd whisper, 'I love you…'

The sun is a honeypot
And my loves a busy bee.
And as you lie here by my side
We are sharing the same dream

And if life was a fairy tale
Every word, would come true
And love would last forever
Thru' these days and nights so blue.

Sail on silver moon, sail on, sail on, sail on,
Sail on silver moon, sail on, sail on, sail on.

When I see a shining flame
Falling thru' the burning night..
I'll always think of you
Wishing everything is so alright, alright.

Sail on silver moon, sail on, sail on, sail on
Sail on silver moon, sail on, sail on, sail on.

I read somewhere you should remember someone at their happiest. It pleases me hugely to be able to say that most of my memories of my Brother are happy ones. Happy, fun times. I do not doubt his love of us. Of me. While he may not have said so directly, it was shown by other means. Inclusion. Not so much in the early years. He was four years my senior after all. But certainly in our adult years. Through the sharing of stories of his vulnerability or when he wanted my opinion on one of his new songs; or of his stories of serendipity where a brief encounter might lead to a professional connection that was beneficial to him. He liked to share that sort of stuff with those close to him.

The last memory I have of my Brother is a happy one. Funny even. And that consoles me. My Brother liked to make us laugh and, ever the joker, he would always make light of his disability.

The moment was snatched really. I was between mom-taxi runs and was rushing from somewhere in Schull to somewhere else in Ballydehob, taking a quick pit stop at my Brother's to check in on the way. Be it guilt or my sub-conscious, but these pit stops were becoming more frequent whenever my Sister-in-Law was away.

Life is made up of interruptions and this one particularly so.

It was the day before he was to die. Unbeknownst to us all.

'Hey Ferg,' I had called out as usual, entering the house expecting to find him either up working on his art, or perhaps in bed as he had been the last few days silently mourning the death of his Music Friend.

'Hey Lyd,' he called back. 'We're in here, I'm just going for a dump.'

So I walked into his room and towards his en-suite to find him mid-air strapped into his hoist and being lowered onto his toilet. My Mother was stood to the side, ever ready to guide and swing him into position over the bowl.

It had become a normal sight. To see him suspended so, with straps securely criss-crossed this way and that, pressing into various parts of his face and neck, arms shoved upwards like featherless wings, his face a dark red due to the blood and air struggle that those crucial few seconds take, gambling life and limb in that moment. A towel is tucked into his t-shirt, bib-like at the chin and draped downwards between his legs to hide any dangly bits.

We are all comfortable in each other's company, each of us having taken turns at different times to assist, hoist, lift and place my Brother. Ever independent, even at the last, he would always man the controls that synchronised his electronic bed, hoist, and automatic toilet.

'How's the head?' I ask, smiling. It is Monday evening following an infamous Sunday night with friends. All gathered with the excuse of discussing and running through the funeral arrangements planned for his Music Friend's service that would follow on the Wednesday.

My Brother is due to sing at this, having chosen to avoid the private Wake or house calling.

Sunday night was by all accounts an emotional, boozy one that ended with some – not my Brother needless to say – skinny dipping in the nearby cove. Despite it being January. I had presumed my Brother would take the usual full day and half to recover from any excesses.

'Oh, I'm fine,' he said, mock indignantly. 'I wasn't drinking.'

I am surprised. In a good way.

'Sure, I can't drink anymore,' he confessed, 'it messes with my meds.'

I had forgotten this fact.

My Mother adjusts his foot so he can get a better balance on the toilet. He offers her the hoist remote. I stay in position at the door-jam as he wobbles on the loo to ground himself.

'I had one with Camilla,' he clarifies. 'Colin's whiskey,' he adds, referring to the bottle that his Music Friend had brought over when he visited the night before his accident, reserved for sharing when they got together again, but never would. 'I started to feel sick even after just that one, so I stuck with water the rest of the night.'

I feel sorry for him and relieved at the same time.

The drink has been a family curse over the decades. It killed my Father's Brother and had been taken up by my own Brother too freely in later years. It is only of late that the drink no longer likes him. He misses it and the social side that goes with it, but he is all the better for not taking it.

'Did you hear about Dad?' he says, laughing.

'No.' I look at my Mother for an explanation. She rolls her eyes at what is to come, but she is also smiling.

Bending forward a little, my Brother releases a rumble of wind and sighs with satisfaction.

We are used to his daily bowel cacophonies, happy for the release it gives him since trapped wind is usually a source of great discomfort and pain for him. *'Better out than in,'* as his Wife would say.

'Dad got langers,' my Brother picks up his story. 'He ferried drink to us all night,' he says, releasing more wind. It reverberates off the toilet basin, dry. No movements yet.

My Mother has turned to his bathroom sink and washes her hands. 'He was dying this morning,' she laughs, looking at me. 'Are you alright there?' she then says, turning to my Brother.

'Yeah,' he says and leans into the room, away from another stream of farts. My Mother makes her way into the kitchen and I can hear her tidying up crockery there. I swivel at the door jamb so that I am now facing into his bedroom and have my back to the bathroom for his added privacy.

'Camilla came over with Steve and Maurice and Maria,' he says.

'Steve?' I draw a name blank.

'Colin's manager,' he says impatiently.

'Oh yeah.' I should know that having met him a few times. 'Is he the blind guy?'

'No,' my Brother tuts.

I conjure up that circle of faces and of whom I think it might be. 'Is it the guy with the beard?'

'Yes,' he says. I hear a splatter interrupted by wind. He grunts with the effort of it.

'How was it?' I ask, actually meaning how it was for my Brother. It was the first time to see his beautiful friend, a Swedish Songbird, since becoming a widow. I imagine it was a very emotional meeting.

'Good, it was good,' he says. 'I gave her a big hug.' He adds. There are more splatters. He sighs with satisfaction. 'A proper hug,' he continues, 'Got her to sit in my lap and to put my arms around her.' There is a pause. 'We both had a good cry.'

I am nodding, my own tears brimming. 'That's lovely,' I manage. 'Good for both of ye.'

'Yeah,' he says. 'It was.'

My Brother is physically unable to hug anymore. He cannot raise his hands high enough himself. Affection is delivered with a joke, a glint in the eye. The family constantly touch him for our contact. A stroke of the arm, a pat on the knee, a kiss on the cheek. We are the ones to lean in to give a hug and get a head nuzzle in return.

I try to recall when I last got an actual hug like that.

It was Christmas day just gone. When he managed to get up, he had to wear his breathing mask the whole time. I joked with him, slagging, calling him *'Darth Vader'*. The elephant in the room was that we were all thinking it would be his last Christmas with us.

When he eventually made it up from his house to my Mother's and we were all gathered in the big room for dinner, he wasn't going to eat with us, no longer able to eat sitting upright. It was a social call. To be part of the tradition. The mask threw us all a bit, so of course I had to make a joke about it.

When he wheeled into the room, I had leant into him and took his arms, placing them up on my shoulders and had to hold them there. He had nuzzled me back, wriggling to empathise his sincerity for the day that was in it.

That was my last hug.

We take so much for granted.

'How did the planning go?' I remember to ask about the whole reason why he was meeting with his friends in the first place.

My Brother laughs. 'We did very little of that.' I hear the sound of the automatic toilet bidet wash, the motor humming along satisfactorily. 'It was a great night though,' he says, laughing again.

'What was so funny about that?' I ask.

My Mother calls out from the kitchen: 'You okay, Ferg?'

'I think I might go again,' he calls back. 'Just a sec, Lyd,' he says to me.

There is the sound of the automatic toilet water spray and purring of the motor.

'Dad brought down wine first,' he says when it is quiet again. There is more wind. He grunts, straining. 'Then when we ran out of that he brought down whiskey and brandy.'

'Oh God,' I laugh.

'We had a great session.' I can hear the joy in my Brother's voice. I can't help but feel a huge sadness for the Songbird. A professional singer in her own right, voice of a spiritual being. Opera, pop, rock, jazz. I do not have the words for her. She lost her Husband, and I have no doubt will remain a true professional in singing at her loved one's funeral service.

I feel it is bittersweet that my Brother and she will have such a great session where both have lost someone loved.

My Brother is laughing again, enjoying the memory of the part of the story he is yet to share.

'Hang on,' he says again. There is more noise of the water pump, spray and flush.

'I'm done, Mom,' he calls out. 'I don't think there is anything else coming.'

'Do you want me to do it?' I ask.

'Nah, you're grand,' he says, huffing with effort. 'Mom'll be faster.'

I take no offence. He is right. When it comes to those in the know-how of hoist slinging and what strap goes where, it is his wife first, then my Mother, then my Sister, with myself and then my Father on the family carers' list. I don't help often enough to remember the correct sequence of the short and the long cross-over or loop that is involved with getting my Brother out of his bed, into the hoist, positioned so he a) doesn't fall out and b) doesn't choke on the straps; and then get him onto the toilet where the routine is swapped to allow for the dance off of towel for privacy and trouser lowering. It is a delicate, practiced skill. Highly choreographed.

'It was the first time where I was the sober one,' my Brother explains, 'and Dad was the one off his face.'

'Why didn't Mom put you to bed?' I ask, looking at my Mother as she passes me to go into my Brother.

'I was gone to bed,' she says matter-of-factly.

'Of course, you were,' I say teasingly. *How stupid of me.* All three of us know that my Mother has a strict policy and low tolerance when it comes to having to wait up beyond midnight to put even her disabled son to bed. Especially if there is drink involved. My Brother's Wife, being much more flexible to such demands, had gone to China and my Sister recently moved to Kinsale. I have my own young family to attend to. So, with my Mother gone to bed, all that remained was my Father.

My Father and Brother in their *last chance saloon.*

My Mother gets into position, adjusting straps and hoist efficiently.

'I was sober, don't forget,' my Brother says, 'giving Dad hoist instructions.' He keeps eye contact with me as my Mother works around him. 'And you know he doesn't follow instructions at the best of times, never mind when drunk.' My Brother titters at the memory of it. 'It was hilarious trying to talk him through what strap goes where.'

My Brother's eyes are glistening with mirth. It is a pleasure to behold. I can't help but laugh myself. 'Are you ready?' my Mother asks, as she hands him the hoist remote.

'Yes,' he says. He looks up to me as he presses the hoist button, raising himself off the toilet bowl. He pauses to allow himself to speak before the lift restricts his breathing and voice.

'Dad was so drunk that he was swinging off the hoist himself until he ended up on the floor. We were both crying with laughter.'

'Jesus, he could have pulled you out of the hoist,' I say, thinking the worst.

'No, no,' he is laughing again. 'I was grand, it was just so funny.' My Brother's laugh has become a mixture of titters and tee-hee-hees. It is contagious. I am laughing with him. For him. At my Father. It feels good. My Mother laughs along with us. It is short-lived, as real time knocks on my mind and, quickly checking my phone, I realise I am late for my Son.

'Shite, I have to go,' I say.

My Mother has already positioned the wheelchair for my Brother, and he is raising himself up, the straps straining on him, and his laugh is pushed out some more. He pirouettes on the one big toe that he can just about master and then pivots towards his chair.

'Are you alright there?' I ask my Mother, still smiling.

'Yes, yes,' she says dismissively.

'Sorry Ferg, I really have to go,' I say, laughing again. 'I have to get Jackson. I'll talk to you tomorrow.'

And I reach out to touch and pat his swinging body, smiling at him as I go. His eyes meet mine, still twinkling.

I did not know it was to be my last contact with him.

I am so so grateful that the last sound I hear from him is his chuckle and more tee-hee-hees as still he feeds off the memory of our Father in drunken hysterics.

My Brother, in that moment, happy.

At least as much as he could have been with his hoist, his porcelain god, and his disability.

At a time when a person might crave privacy, Irish tradition knows better.

When other nations and people might choose family-only affairs, the Celtic way is of celebration and gathering. There is a lot to be said for it. We snatch private moments, and these are good for reflection, to grieve, to re-boot. But there is a lot to be said for being surrounded by friends and family at a time of hypersensitivity and vulnerability.

The Irish do not hush death. We greet it full on and welcome it with open arms. On one condition. As long as it is someone else's.

My Brother's life, and death, was such a celebration. We marked his passing as much as his living. Full on. As grief-struck as I am, I remind myself that he had reached a point in life where he no longer looked forward. Life had become a struggle. Maybe it really was his time to go. And on the scale of things, with the best scenario being that of going in his sleep, this unexpected death is probably the second best. Better than tied up in a hospital bed with tubes and nappies and machines, with his mind trapped in a wasting body. No, this was better, if not best. This way there was no human intervention. The decision, any decision, was taken out of human hands. Call it luck, divine intervention, the universe. Call it what you may. In any case, it is for the better.

It is hard to acknowledge that it was a 'happy release' as I step out of the pew and follow his casket down the aisle outside.

The weather wraps around the church, tears of rain slashing at the main portico.

Realising that his parasol would not live through the torrent, I take the little umbrella off the casket and step aside from the cortege in order to fold it before I would join my family outside again.

As I struggle with the mechanics of the delicate keepsake my Daughter is soon at my side, and now we are two man-handling the device. More pass, walking now beyond us leaving a respectful gap, eyes acknowledging the struggle but convention compelling them out into the weather after my Brother. My Husband's Brother-in-Law steps in and with brute force has the umbrella folded and back in my hand. I am laughing again. *Is it you Ferg? Is it you ensuring that there will be little moments of slapstick to get me through the day?*

Tucking his folded poetry under my own jacket, I step out into reality, the rain pin pricking my face and pecking at my shoulders. There is something amiss at the hearse. Some gather, embarrassed looking, at the open car door, others are shuffling off towards the hotel or to the nearest watering hole. The wind pulls at my jacket, and I pinch it closer to protect the parasol.

I find my Sister with her arm around my distraught Sister-in-Law.

'What's up?' I ask quietly, guessing that more than grief has affected my Brother's Wife.

'She thought Fergus would be brought into the hotel for the gig.'

Ah Jesus.

My Sister-in-Law looks to me pleading: 'Ferr' no go to hotel?'

I shake my head, devastated for her. How could we have been so stupid not to have talked her through the various stages? Explain our Irish ways. How could we have presumed that she would know? How could she?

'No, Li,' I say softly. 'He'll go up to Arundel's, the funeral home.' I nod towards the hill-top of the town.

'Alone?' she asks.

I nod again.

'I go with him,' she announces.

My Sister hugs her more tightly around the shoulders. 'You can't Li. It is closed after. No one allowed in. Ferg will rest there.'

'No,' she demands. 'He no be alone. I go.' She goes to move and my Sister's grip tightens. In the same moment I touch her shoulder to get her to look me in the eye. 'Everyone is going to the hotel. All Ferg's friends will be there. Great music, party. His party.'

She turns to look down the street through the rain, through her tears. There is a stream of people darting towards the hotel still. Some with jackets held over heads, others hunched away from the wet.

'Party?'

'Yes, Li,' my Sister says. 'For Fergus. Glen will sing again, and Liam and Maria.'

'Ferr' will miss music,' she says pityingly.

'He will hear them up the street, Li,' my Sister says.

'Yes,' I agree enthusiastically. 'It will be such a great party that the whole town will hear it.' I say it almost joyfully. We both turn her away from the hearse. 'Ferg would want you to be there,' I add, hoping.

This is enough to convince her. I do not see the Pillars close the door of the hearse. I choose not to. There is that part of me too that wants to go with my Brother and sit with him. But I am cold and getting very wet. The hotel lights and trail of friends heading that way are a greater lure. The practical part of me wants to follow.

If my Brother were here, he would be ahead of me already, his chair whirring, wheels spraying road-spit up his useless legs and he, leaning into the wind and rain, probably laughing, anticipating a great night ahead of him. While his corpse may lie in the casket, I know he is no longer there. I imagine his spirit is already at the hotel, centre of attention, mixing in with the crowd. Delighted at the turn out and having a good laugh at his own expense. There will be many who will be buying him one for the road tonight.

At first, I make my way towards the function room. This has a separate entrance to the side of the hotel, and I trail in out of the rain. I have lost my Sister-in-Law and Sister somewhere along the way. The corridor has been decorated with borrowed easels upon which sit my Brother's artwork. Shiny jam jars filled with night light candles light up the floor beneath. Wild flowers sit in vases and jugs at every second one. I am moved. Sadness creeps up from my belly, and I don't want to dally.

I hear the crowd ahead of me. Pushing in the double doors to the main room, I am hit with a wall of sound and heat. The room is throbbing. The atmosphere is jubilant. There are walls of familiar faces. Long unseen friends are hugging each other. The bar is bustling as staff hurry orders and there are calls for pints, shorts and minerals.

I scan the crowd to try and find my Husband, my Father, my own friends. I don't want to be here in this room with these people. With this energy. Somewhat pleased with the liberation of this decision, I turn on my heel and make my way into the hotel bar. It is quieter here, still busy, but the energy is more subdued. As luck would have it, there is a free high table in a corner against a wall with a comfortable looking high padded seat that is fixed, facing out to the room. I decide that it is here I will ensconce myself. My mouth is parched and I feel now is the time for a Barcardi and coke. A large one. My heart rises when I recognise the back of two of my Dublin friends. We go back a-ways, to days of courting, hanging out, marriage, property climbing, children making, shared hangovers and crass jokes. Miscarriages, failed businesses, late night laughter and long catch up calls. This would be our first funeral together.

I tap their shoulder and each in turn reaches for me and I relish the genuine warm embrace and whisper kisses. He is now at the bar, calling over his shoulder, guessing correctly my chosen tipple and soon she has me sat at the high table. I feel safe; exhausted, numb, but safe.

'Oh Lydia, the service was beautiful,' she gushes.

I nod, tears welling again. I grip her hand. 'Thank you so much for coming.'

'Oh, not at all. You know us, wouldn't miss a good party.' Her eyes are moist too, the striking blue accentuated by her auburn hair. I love her for her wit and humour, and being here. Another link soldered.

He saunters over, hands burdened with slim-jims clinking with ice and swimming lemons.

'Just what the doctor ordered,' I say, giving him a weak smile.

'I ordered you a double,' he says, with a cheeky grin. 'I thought you might need it.'

I nod, and we toast my Brother. I gulp one and then a second sup. I feel the lemony sweet syrup pricked with glorious sting glide down the back of my throat and pass through my chest. It dissipates my cloud some and drops into my stomach. My body relaxes, shoulders round and sucking in a long slow breath; my belly softens.

The inevitable storytelling of my Brother's death has to be shared. They knew him well enough to deserve the detail. Omitting what I promised I would not tell. Inside I struggle with holding back. These are my friends, and I have shared many, often too many, a secret with them. But now we have a Family Secret, and it is sacred. I couldn't. Wouldn't. I will not be the one to let the cat out of the bag. I will wait for another to do that.

Telling what I can is therapeutic. And, timing just right, my Friend who travelled from America comes in flagged by another boarding schoolfriend, my K-Girl Buddy. Hugs and kisses again shared. I may be the common denominator, but this circle of friends have known each other too over the years. Linking up at different gatherings, around special birthdays and two very memorable New Year's Eves.

I am on auto pilot and sit on the high seat with my Friend from America sat next to me and my other friends sitting around me. Like in Auden's poem, being my North, my South, my East, and my West.

My true Compass.

In this moment I feel grounded, relaxed even. Secure.

Others come and go into the hotel bar, local friends, acquaintances. All pass through, travelling as if on a parallel jet stream of alcohol, fanfare, and reunion to the big room where the rock-n-roll scene unfurls. Their energy is too high for me to join in. I am very happy where I sit. Flanked by my guardians.

My Brother's Archivist Friend, my "Step-Brother", comes into the bar, eyes scanning the room, and, on seeing me, makes his way over with purpose. 'Lyd. Come inside. Glen is jamming with Liam and Mundy. The music is amazing.'

I am allergic at the thought of leaving my cocoon and enter the hive of activity.

'Oh Marc, I am really comfy here.' I look around at my friends.

'You should show your face at least,' he says gently. 'People are looking for you.'

Social obligation. *Damn it.* Haven't I done everything correct so far. Ticked all the boxes. There is no precedence in my life skills for something like this bit. A live gig with the famous, post funeral. I am not a musician. Never been part of my Brother's circle that way. Why start now? I feel it would be pretentious. Hypocritical. Let someone else do it. And then I skip through my family and know my Mother will have already slipped away after the funeral, guess that my Sister-in-Law may have done the same, and wonder where my Father and Sister are.

I'm about to ask when guilt and responsibility kick in. It is my Brother's party after all. He is not here himself and, like my Compass friends, most have travelled distances to be here. I owe them some contact at least.

'Okay, okay,' I say, slipping off the high seat, sliding my hands down my hips to adjust my dress. 'Don't let them take my drink,' I caution the circle.

'I'll order you a backup,' my Dublin Pal winks at me. I smile back and lean in to give him a firm kiss on his cheek, squeezing his shoulder. Words aren't needed.

Walking towards the function room I can feel the base throbbing before I hear it. The double doors burst outwards towards me as someone scurries to the toilets, and a wave of guitar, vocals, heat, and smell of sweat greet me. I have lost track of the time but it feels late, like the afters of a wedding. The crowd surges on the dance floor, all eyes on the stage. I recognise the Oscar Winner and his Irish speaking singing companion but the others I can't put names to the faces. There is a wave of arms held high as palms and phones pay homage to the musician gods.

To my right are table rounds full of people sitting, leaning in towards each other as they catch up over the din. The bar is still two rows deep. All around me I see familiar faces and don't know who to select. I have to pick as I won't just stand here, the odd one unmoving amidst the pulsating crowd. I am not drunk enough to just jump right in. I feel totally sober, clear headed. Heavy hearted, but still clear headed. I decide I should drink some water anyway and make for the bar.

Everybody, the entire room, is here for my Brother. No, that is not entirely true. They are also here for us. My Parents, my family, my Sister-in-Law, for me. For themselves. For each other.

The Secret jumps into my mind again. None of them know. They think he went naturally. That it was his time. Lung failure or something medical. It eats at me. Not like a Great White tearing chunks but as short sharp quick bites. Like piranha. Only it is not a school of them. It is only one. Swimming secretly around in my belly with its own private pool in my chest, nip picking here and there at my honesty box.

Someone passes me, '*Whoop Whoop!*' Calling out: 'Ferg would love this.' And raises his glass in toast, spilling some liquid onto the shoulder of another unsuspecting passer-by. They, oblivious, smile at me, raising their hand in a wave, already facing forward again towards the musicians.

I push through the crowd, smiling at one, nodding at another. The crowd is weaving together now in unison at the familiar song. I know it, but yet don't. I spot my Sister in the middle of one line. Shoulder to shoulder, her arms around the waist of those either side of her and they in turn linked to her. There is an unspoken message relayed through the crowd and another joins the line, then another and another. A second line is formed, then a third. I step back away from them, subtly rejecting any arms that are raised to engulf blindly those next to them. I do not feel drawn towards this kinship of energy.

The lines remind me of teen céilís and family weddings, where the band would call for the Walls of Limerick. Others rush from the tables to feed off this united energy, to join in on the lines. Celtic spirit, brothers and sisters in arms, in drink, in unison. In grieving. The lines pulsing like waves ebb and flow on the shore. I see my Father along the way. His shirt and brow soaked in sweat. Cheeks aglow, he is beaming and singing along with the chorus as are all within the room. I can see there is in that moment a happiness. Mindful of that snapshot, I capture it in my mind's eye. I scan the crowd for my Sister and she too is laughing, cheering, joyous. It is heart-warming to witness. But I don't feel it. I see it. I acknowledge it; their happiness feeding a small pocket in my heart where I will keep it precious, to bring up again when I need to call on it.

Content that I have been in the room as requested, have shown my face, that I am not needed, I withdraw into the hall, leaving the throbbing mass, and retreat back into the bar. Pushing the door in, I look to my high seat and corner spot, hoping that I have not lost my space and companions. I am relieved to see that, not only is it still unoccupied but remains flanked by my own friends in arms. Waiting, protecting, keeping, all looking at me, smiling that smile reserved and understood by true friends of old. A coded Celtic silent welcome built into our DNA.

There you are. Come on in, sit by the fire. The kettle is on, the fire is lit, sure aren't we going nowhere but here for yourself.

My Husband's Brother approaches the table. Politely greets my friends, his acquaintances. I feel my neck tense. He is one half, the other, his wife, is not here. My Husband's family representation has met social etiquette. A representation of each of his siblings' families have made the journey. My Husband is one of six. To include spouses and children brings the numbers into the twenties. It is not practical to have everyone come.

Looking at my Husband's Brother, I can't help but feel a disappointment, a rejection, because his wife, my friend, chose not to come. The feeling rises in me and, while I know it is not his doing, I am curt and almost dismissive with him. I am not impolite, but I do not engage him. I cannot make eye contact. What was it he had said when my Husband had asked why his wife wouldn't make it? 'Isn't it enough that there is a family representation?' A family representation.

In contrast, my K-buddy who I have not seen in five years has dropped her own stressful and busy working mothering life to be here for me. And I feel the love from her. It radiates from her smile, her eyes. Spreads from her core into mine. Once more I look around the circle and tell myself it is enough. I am loved. As my Brother was loved. He me, and I him. Love. Love for family and love for friends. My chest cavity warms, and my ribs lift off my stomach. I reach for my K-Buddy's hand and squeeze it gently. She smiles and squeezes back. Words not needed. No words.

My Oldest Girlfriend and her Young Husband, taking a short cut through the bar from the street, find us at the table. Spotting me, she walks towards me theatre style, leading with a rounded shoulder, her head tilted and with a blaggard glint in her bloodshot eyes. I recognise the gait enough to know that she is well on. The rogue within her has awoken. Her Young Husband follows behind at a stagger, grinning as if it is Christmas morning. Buzzing on a natural high. While the reason for the get together is a sad one, I guess that he is still in awe of the talent and showmanship that has gathered in the one place. And that is okay. I take no offence at the energy steaming from him. He has a right to be here. He is not just any *plus one*. Grief has visited him already at a young age, having lost his own father at fifteen. And my Oldest Girlfriend has had it tough of late, caring, along with her sister, for her mother speckled with cancer. I can't help but smile, feeling they both have a licence to let their hair down and enjoy the celebration.

Why is that? Why do I afford a permission to some to be loose and free and celebrate, and to others resent their participation, or lack thereof?

'Awcomeon,' she slurs at me across the bar table, 'willyanotcomein? The musssik is greatsh.' She sways on the spot, raising her arm to beckon me with her index finger and winks an unfocused eye.

'Ah no, I'm good here hun.'

Her energy is high. Party mood. While I have no difficulty with her celebratory energy, I am allergic to the thought of jumping into the mix.

Her Husband sways quietly behind her. Hand in his pockets, eye darting towards the door and back to the circle. He smiles at me on making eye contact.

'You go on in and enjoy,' I add, 'Seriously, I'm very happy here.' I look to my Compass again. My Oldest Girlfriend pulls a mock pout and, smiling again, I shake my head at her. Her eyes suddenly dart in another direction, and I follow her gaze to see who has distracted her.

It is my Oldest Pal with his Husband in tow. There are happy greetings between those in the circle and brief introductions to the newly acquainted spouses. My Old Pal is not happy looking; his face lacks genuine animation and his mouth is turned down just at the edges. I sense that he is about to tell me that they are leaving.

'We're going to go,' he confirms.

'But you can't go,' I lament. 'I haven't had a chance to talk to you at all.' Now it's my turn to pout. How did I not seek him out earlier?

'I want to stay,' he says, 'but Toni....' He doesn't finish the sentence. There is the old air in it, like when we were kids and he had lost out to the decision maker and we had to end the game in the middle of a great bit. Would have to miss out.

Hoping my plea might win his Husband over, I slide out of my seat. 'Oh Toni, would ye not stay a bit longer?' My pal's Husband looks sheepishly at me but doesn't answer.

'It has all been a bit much for him I think,' my Old Pal explains.

I understand it is useless. Another instinct. I know my Old Pal long enough to know that look. Any negotiation or pleading is fruitless. The decision has been made.

'Derm, willyanot stay? Stay for a drink,' my unsteady Oldest Girlfriend asks, throwing a jelly-arm around him. I see his shoulders stiffen. Not out of any disdain for her, they know each other of old too, all three of us being primary school friends. But he has never liked conflict or is uncomfortable with conforming to the crowd. He had to fight his own corner long enough. There are feeble efforts by the Compass to convince them otherwise and I feel him grow even more tense.

'Ah, no, he is good,' I say. 'Come on, I'll walk ye out.'

'Wait,' my blue-eyed auburn Dublin Friend calls. 'We have to get a photo. Of the old gang.' She looks about the circle. 'When was the last time we were all together?'

And I realise she is right. Besides my two old primary school friends' respective Husbands, all of us have not been together as one for many years. There have been odd occasions where one or two were missing, but there is just one other time that we were all gathered together as now. A motley crew of friends with myself as the common dominator.

'Oh my God, you're right,' my Friend from America says.

'What year was that?' another asks.

'It was that New Year's Eve,' I say, warming as the memory rises. 'Same place, different time. 1989-90?'

'What?' someone else asks, incredulous. Someone else shrieks joyfully.

I am laughing. 'It is almost thirty years ago.' We are all laughing now as we gravitate towards each other, hug shoulders, and someone is given an iPhone to capture the historic moment. I am stood in the centre of them all, secure in their embrace. I feed off their happy energy, their shared kinship. My Brothers and Sisters in arms. My Walls of Limerick.

I think of my Brother and how bittersweet it is that it has taken his death to bring us back together again.

SUNDAY

February 7

Sunday is a day of goodbyes. Folk must get on the road again, return to their normality. Ours will never be the same. We will have a new normal.

In any case we are not done yet. There is still the cremation to attend tomorrow.

And today, the family must all say goodbye to my Brother's stepson.

There was confusion with days and timing. Because the funeral was Saturday, my Step-Nephew had presumed the cremation would be Sunday. Had booked his flights accordingly. Communication fails again.

We had all been surprised to learn that the crematorium does not open on a Sunday. I suppose cremators are entitled to their days off too. And so, Monday was the earliest for us. My Step-Nephew's tickets to Japan could not be changed without great expense, and his time off work was limited. My Brother was not his Father, after all – from a Japanese HR point of view anyway. So he would make his way to Dublin today for an early flight tomorrow, back to Japan and work. My Sister-in-Law would travel as far as Dublin with him.

'Why is she going too?' my Sister asks. 'She should be here.'

'I dunno. Maybe to see him off?' I say, nipping a sarcastic tone.

'What about the cremation?' she grumbles.

I look to my Husband for reason.

'She's going to get an early train down on Monday, and I will meet her off it,' he explains. 'Mick and Niamh are bringing them up to Dublin today,' he continues, 'so Mick will make sure she gets the train on time tomorrow.'

'Is she staying with them so?' my Sister asks more calmly

'Yes.'

'Oh, right so.'

'Poor Deng,' I say. 'It's awful he's going to miss Monday.' I look out the kitchen window that gives a clear view across the Bridge of Woe to the house below. I see the car at the ready, doors and boot open, packed up for a great exodus.

'I suppose we should go down and say our goodbyes,' I suggest.

I can't help but feel a great sadness for my Step-Nephew.

Having arrived in this country at the age of 15 from the heart of mainland China, 'a small city of eight million', the West was such a shock for him. '*Where has the water gone*?' he had asked at the wonder of the ocean's tide.

I can't imagine what it must have been like in the early days for him: the emotional and psychological skills needed to cope with both the culture and societal habits of us westerners. Europeans. Irish. Mix in a rock-n-roll *cripple* for a stepfather. Hats off to him.

I have no doubt though that my Brother won him over and gave him a refreshing perspective on life and living, a perspective that no able-bodied Father could. The love and respect followed quickly, and the mutual regard between the two was evident in later years.

My Step-Nephew stood stoic and quiet the whole week; if he had any inner turmoil it was not evident. Keeping face. He reserved his extended family's feelings for the church podium during the Celebration, when, with great pride and Chinese honour, he read out a personal message from his own family in China. His grandfather, the patriarch of my Sister-in-Law's side, had written a message for us, and my Step-Nephew had translated it. My own Father felt it was appropriate that it should be read out at the funeral.

And the mantle to be assumed by my Step-Nephew:

'All of us – the family of Fergus, of Li in China and overseas, are deeply saddened by the news. We would like to send our deepest condolences.

When we received the news, some were crying, some were numb but all of us were thinking of Fergus. There were many family members showing their respect to Fergus, we will all remember Fergus forever.

Fergus was always so kind and full of love for his friends and family. He is stronger than most people, full of determination and creativity, always learning new things and achieved so much in his music and arts. People love his arts and his music will be played in Ireland, in China and all over the world.

To our dearest Fergus:

Your kindness to the family will always be remembered;

Your smile and soulful voice will always be remembered;

Your art will be hanged on the wall in our house and be looked at every day;

Your music will always be listened by us and shared by the world.

Rest in peace, our dearest Fergus.

No matter where you are, your lovely wife will always be thinking of you. I'll always remember when we first met, Li was driving us through beautiful Ireland whilst listening to your music. It was such a wonderful and romantic time.

Rest in peace, our dearest Fergus.

No matter where you are, your family in China and all over the world will always remember you fondly, respect you and learn from you. You will always be the most popular one no matter where you are, people will always welcome you with open arms, hug you and love you. Goodbye our dearest Fergus. You will always live in our hearts.

From the family Fergus and Li in China and oversea' 孟

My Sister-in-Law has to see her only son and child off to the airport. To say a different goodbye. She will be left alone. Of course there is us, but it is not the same, is it? We are not blood. We are her token family. As politically correct we might like to be, the reality is that we cannot give her what her son can. We cannot give her what my Brother gave her.

I feel a huge sense of loneliness for her.

The house below is like a train station where the last of the carriages prepares to depart. There is a small glut of bodies queuing at the door with bags and arms hanging loose for hugs.

My Brother's Documentary Making Friend and his other half are still packing their car. Searching for pockets of space to cram in the last of the bags and baggage. Even the car's rear window is stuffed with pillows, child's blankets and toys.

Glancing into the car interior, I see there is barely room for legs never mind the rest of them.

'Where are you going to fit everybody?' I ask jokingly.

'Ah sure, we'll squeeze them in somehow,' he quips.

My Step-Nephew comes out laden with a large heavy looking bag and his mother follows behind blabbering Chinese instructions. I sense tension and stress and guess that pre-travel anxiety is already building. The Documentary Making Friend magics up some space to fit the bag into the boot. 'What have you got in this?' he mocks, 'it weighs a tonne.'

'Ye'r' off so?' I say, attempting to keep it light, but a lump catches in my throat and the 'so' ends in a croak. It's best if I don't say any more and I step in to give my Step-Nephew a hug. I have no idea when I am going to see this young man again. While it is nice to think that he will visit, the reality is that it is easier for his mother and him to meet in China and catch up there with their own clan. He squeezes me back and neither of us say anything. I hug the others and find that I am welling up again.

'Keep in touch,' I manage, and it is not long before they have done the rounds, the goodbyes, and the car is heading down the drive. I watch as it leaves us and smile as an arm appears from the driver's side to wave frantically. I wave in return, blindsided on seeing the warped face of a teddy stare back at me through the back screen of the car.

The big room in the main house is busy with people and the makings of another banquet. A leftovers one. Bludgeoned honey roast ham rules the table with a melting cheese board, muddy looking potato salad, crumbled brown soda, half eaten bowls of quinoa and couscous, wilting organic green salad, and asymmetric butter. Crescent moon apple tarts, cheesecake, a defrosted pie. Multi half bottles of white and red wine left at either end, alongside wrapped cutlery and messy jars of condiments.

It is as if the feast itself is hungover and exhausted from the night before. All laid out for the weary travellers to use up, if willing, before long journeys home towards Cork, Dublin, and beyond.

People chat animatedly. There is normal talk of travel arrangements, journey lengths, and return to work, and so on. Last minute catch-ups by those missed during the gathering.

I feel tired and pour myself a large glass of white, taking a slab of crumbling soda bread, smearing it with a blanket of butter, stacking it with clove-spotted, fat-trimmed ham slice, and spooning on a thin veil of mustard. Taking the first bite, I feel my cheeks fill with saliva. I am famished. I have not eaten much in the last few days. I sit and enjoy the combination of flavours that conjure up a feeling of Saint Stephen's day and post-Christmas contentment. Served up with a dollop of sadness.

The big room is a meeting point. For evaluation. Review. Some sitting and eating, others taking coffee or tea standing, others again hovering, needing to leave but not relinquishing just yet; come and go they must. The morning shifts into lunch time and then on into the afternoon. There are many goodbyes. My Friend from America, my Dublin friends, my In-Laws, my aunts and uncles, my hungover Oldest Girlfriend and her suffering Young Husband, they all arrive to pay their final compliments, gratitude, and farewell.

And then it is time.

That is what it does.

Time moves on.

We have no control over that.

The air is filled with the knock-knocking of life's door. The need to leave takes over from the want to stay, and I am forced to stand. To hug. To escort to cars. To say goodbye to my old K-Buddy who must return to her own mothering working world. Not before the chemist in her advises me on the creeping infection on my cheek. Gratefully received.

It is hardest to say goodbye to my Dublin friends who will also bring my Friend from America with them to visit her aging mother before travelling onward to New York. To stand as car doors are shut and hands wave from behind glass and then step away from reversing cars, walk around u-turns and move to be in sight of rear view mirrors, all the time hands waving and eyes brimming. The drive empties.

At the last.

The inevitable.

It is just me and my own left behind.

'Did your Father tell you about the bird?' my Mother asks.

It is evening time. Night has cloaked us. We are sitting in the quiet of the kitchen, my Mother making lists at her desk as she smokes another fag while I look over Facebook again.

'Bird? No,' I say, not bothering to look up.

'A bird flew into his office and sat up on his dresser,' she says mockingly.

'Seriously?' I sit up straight, logging out of Facebook, curious now.

'Yah, came in the door there,' she says, pointing at the patio door. 'Flew down to your Father's office. Your Father wouldn't move it so I shooed it out.'

'What!' I stand and go to move when my Father comes into the kitchen. 'Dad, what's this about a bird?' I say, incredulous.

He looks to my Mother and back to me again. He smiles. 'Yes, a little sparrow came in and flew down the hall into my office.'

'A sparrow – not a robin?' (Robins are known to be adventurous and explore houses)

'Yeah, a sparrow. And I wouldn't mind but it was after sunset,' he says, eyes glinting. He is using his *Daddy* voice, the one reserved for affectionate banter with his youngest. 'When all the little birds would normally be asleep in their nests.' His tone is comforting and familiar.

'I was in my office when he flew in and perched up on the TV dresser, looking down on me.' His voice has returned to normal. Happy normal. 'You know Ferg bought that TV for me.'

'Oh my God.' The hair rises on the back of my neck, and I am tickled with happiness as it crawls under my skin and spreads over me. I know where this is going, and I love it.

'It was Ferg,' I declare, laughing, clapping my hands. 'What did you do?'

'I didn't do anything. Left him alone. He was happy there. And I liked him being there,' he says smiling. 'Looking down on me as I worked away.'

I look over to my Mother who rolls her eyes. 'Your Father came in about half an hour later and told me about it. Thought he got the bird out but then he told me it was still there.'

I glance back to my Father. We are both smiling.

'Your Mother got rid of it,' he said then.

'Mu-um!' I say, mock disapprovingly.

'Well, I didn't want it shitting everywhere. On your Father's carpet,' she huffs. 'I just turned off all the lights except the porch light. Had to clap my hands to get him out and led it back down the hall out the front door.'

I am full of wonder. 'When he flew in from the patio, was the door to the big room open?'

'I suppose,' my Mother says, before taking a sip of coffee. 'It usually is.'

'Sure, he could have gone in there, or up the stairs to the landing. Or just flapped about the kitchen.'

My Mother is looking blankly at me. My Father is still smiling.

'So he came in the door, had to leave the kitchen, turned right instead of left, flew down the darker hallway instead of towards the light of the big room, and found dad's office? Perched on his dresser and stayed there looking down at you? Didn't flap about the place in a panic?'

My Father is laughing now.

'It was Ferg,' I say, loving the magic in it. Doesn't matter if it is all superstition or chance. Or a sign. The serendipity of it is just too wonderful. My Brother not dead a week and a bird finds its way specifically into my Father's office and watches over him for a while. It has brought laughter. Sparked something inside. Got us wondering. Questioning.

My Brother loved serendipity. Found it throughout life. Saw it in many places. At many times. Maybe it is us just reaching for the positive. Seeing two things that happen at the same time and putting them together to help us justify a coincidence.

My Mother brushes it off. 'It was just a bird,' she says tutting. But still she is smiling.

You couldn't make it up.

I take note of empty spaces around my Brother's house. His Mac is gone. So is all the hanging artwork. Even some framed paintings. It is only when my Sister-in-Law is gone that I realise that possessions have also vanished.

'Li took them with her,' my Sister explains.

'Even the Big Mac?' I ask astonished. While none of my Brother's things are ours, I am surprised that his wife has already removed them from the house.

'Are you sure it is not upstairs?'

'Why do you think Deng Li's bag was so heavy?' my Sister says, smoking her cigarette. 'She gave it to him to bring back to Japan.'

'Are you serious?' I am dumbstruck. 'But that has Ferg's business stuff on it, and his music.'

'She took the artwork with her too.'

'All of it?'

My Sister nods, blowing the cigarette smoke upwards towards the ceiling. I am guessing my Sister is not at all surprised.

'Shit.'

'Sure, she was handing out all sorts to people as they were leaving.'

'Jesus.' And then I think back to her gifting my Brother's tux jacket to my Daughter. Is it a Chinese thing to pass on to others items that will help the memory of Brother live on? Her way of sharing his love. Regardless of any of my Brother's wishes. Regardless of his will.

Inwardly I panic. 'What did she do with the boots?'

'Oh she left those for you.' My Sister takes a sip of her water. 'They are still down in the house.'

I leave my Sister and find myself hurrying to my Brother's and seeking out his boots. I can't see them, and panicking, scurry from one room to the next trying to find them. Fearing they have been taken back to Japan, or worse, thrown out. They may be ready for the bin, but I want them. They are more than boots to me. I see them sitting on the floor under his desk. The mock shins and wooden shelf still intact. I grab them up as if they might run away from me. Once in my arms I feel myself relax. Already I imagine a spot for them at home. With the teardrop urn containing his ashes sitting upon them nicely. They will make a quirky shrine. My Brother should be comfortable there.

MONDAY

February 8

Christ's hour comes round again: the cremation planned for three o'clock.

We will follow my Brother's hearse to Cork, travelling in small groups in different cars, my Eldest accompanying her Grandfather leading behind the hearse, me driving my Mother's car with her as a passenger and my Daughter and Son in the back, my Sister driving with her husband and family. My Husband has returned to work in the city, already having left at dawn. He will meet my Sister-in-Law there.

It is another miserable morning with the West Cork drizzle being persistent and stubborn. We are pulled up outside the village funeral home that is located out of sight up a side road off the main street of Schull. We double park and wait. It has already been decided who will move my Brother from the funeral home to the hearse, and I look on from within the car.

This is his last moment in Schull.

Snatching glimpses through the junction to the main street beyond, I spy villagers as they cross unaware of this moment. I wonder will the village carry out the tradition of closing doors, pulling blinds, and switching off lights as we go by. How often have I stood still in the dark of a village main street store to pay respects to the passing dead and now we are on the other side.

My Brother settled in the hearse, it moves off at a slow, gentle pace. We all follow in the respective cars. We are a small convoy.

The village is quiet, the street vacant. Not out of respect but because it is a Monday morning in February. Doors are closed. If businesses are open for trading it is only evident by raised blinds and lights on. We pass through the village and out the other side and I am saddened that my Brother has had to leave this way. Unnoticed. Business as usual.

Traders unaware that he passes, tucked in away from the damp grey cloud that lingers over the village and tenderly strokes our cars as we trail through.

I am driving and consciously register the journey. Mindful. Keeping a close distance from my Father's car, as he does in turn to the hearse. I talk to my Brother in my head. *Are you okay? Are you comfortable? Are you even journeying with us or off somewhere else, oblivious?* I am deeply saddened that his form is leaving West Cork for the last time. Abandoning the capital and his rock-n-roll life, it was his choice to move to this seaside town. In the interest of his love for life and his love for his wife.

'If you are going to marry Li,' my Mother had cautioned back in the day, 'and move her from Cyprus to here, you will have to change your lifestyle. You can't expect her to move here to your crazy life of living by night and sleeping by day.'

That was over twenty years ago, and he had moved. Changed his pattern. Still composed, and created, even partied. But with his wife in the mix. Both learning to live a life that all marriages must. A balance of living the life that keeps you either sane or wonderfully insane. Now he leaves that all behind. Leaves us. Alone. Starts another adventure.

We make our way to the city, skirting it with the by-pass and, somewhere along the route, I realise my mind has wandered and I no longer know where I am and don't know how to get to the crematorium. I am anxious to keep my Father's taillights in sight, impatient at other cars that slip in-between me and him and junctions along the way. I am conscious that my Sister's car is relying on me to know where I am going, as much as I am reliant on my Father's.

Acknowledging that negative thoughts and feelings are surfacing, I put my trust in the universe, in my Brother, convincing myself that I am worrying unnecessarily. We will all get there together. And we do.

It has been arranged that my Husband would leave work to pick up my Sister-in-Law from the train, and when we pull up, they are already parked and standing in the slippery weather, waiting. Having parked, and pulling on my own coat, I go to them now and greet my Sister-in-Law first, then my Husband, giving him a hug and a kiss.

'How is she?' I ask, out of her earshot.

'As well as you can expect,' he says, pulling his own coat around himself. I nod, not knowing what else to say.

Two polished-looking Pillars dressed in black come forward from the Crematorium main entrance to greet us. I recognise one as our West Cork funeral directors and find myself relaxing on seeing a familiar face.

There is no script or stage direction that comes with such things, and for a moment I have no idea what happens next. Hanging back, my focus now moves towards my Son. Guilty of having as good as forgotten that he has existed in the last week; sporadically checking his presence, that he is safe, that he has eaten. The bare minimum. I hug him to me as we both watch the Pillars, my Eldest, my Niece, and the family men carry my Brother inside.

We are on an island. Emotionally and physically. We have removed ourselves from civilisation and the city and have crossed a wide modern bridge. It is the final leg, where we bring my Brother to the end. I feel it is metaphoric to have been led here to this small rock at Cork's harbour where we cross a bridge and now have nowhere else to go. A dreary looking ending. The view from the island is of an industrial estate across the bay, the modern bridge and the harbour water. Not exactly pretty, and the slush-like swipe of grey cloud and misty drizzle does not help with the aesthetics. My eye does not dawdle long as it is drawn to the cortege that now lumbers away from us and so I follow.

I am pleasantly surprised by the paved path that meanders under an historic granite arch. It reminds me of the granite arches that are also in my old alma mater, Kylemore Abbey, and I am immediately walking through a blasted bedrock tunnel that leads on into a magnificent courtyard. An air of stillness and calm oozes now instead of ominous weaponry and destruction that once served this island's magazine. The courtyard is enclosed, flanked by some hundred feet of natural rock face on one side and on the other, a stone-faced one-storey building that has large curved glass arches for windows and entrance. It is a pleasant contrast to the bleak exterior.

A wind blows through the courtyard, flirting with planted bamboo, and energising the air around us. Whispers are carried into us, and my Sister-in-Law appears delighted, smiling and turning a circle on the spot. Twirling. 'It always like this?' she asks one of the Pillars.

'No, it was a magazine for storing gunpowder back in its day.'

I see her frown at his explanation. He has misunderstood her question.

'No, I think she means is it usually windy in here?' I explain.

She and I both look upward, and the rock face frames the sky perfectly. A rock pool of the sky. The weather appears so far away. Mottled clouds scud across the mucky sky while a soft rain gusts overhead. The wet does not filter downward. Only the dry wind dances around us, whipping our coats and teasing loose tendrils of our hair.

'No,' he answers, 'that's unusual alright. With the rock formation the wind usually blows straight over the island, not through it like this.'

My Sister-in-Law is delighted.

'Baliama,' she beams and stamps her foot. 'It is Ferr'. He here.'

I smile, as I am happy to go along with believing it too. It is as if my Brother approves.

Bamboo, curving paths set into cobbled courtyard; a water feature and sculpture of a heron, sensitive to all religious and none; stained glass windows and curved doorways; and then we are in.

The room is wider than it is long and rows of seats curve in a crescent, facing double sliding doors inlaid with curved wrought ironwork and modern stained glass that mirrors that at the entrance. And there he is: my Brother's casket is sat up on a ledge in a raised alcove, centre stage between the two sliding panels. Unlike in the movies, where we see the foot of a casket, or coffin, my Brother's is laid horizontal to us, and my Sister-in-Law instinctively walks up close and places her hand on its edge.

Our small group hardly fills the front row, never mind the room, and we hover, not sure what is to happen next. None of us sit.

There is a movement in the corner of the room and my Brother's Sound Engineer Friend walks towards us. I am surprised to see him here. For a moment I resent that this non-family member is with us at this very private moment, and I talk reason to myself on seeing him squat down to a music system and speakers.

I understand now.

He has come to set up music for my Brother so at his last we could say farewell with a song which we are all most familiar. He explains that he has set up my Brother's own 'Sail On' to play, and when we are ready to hit the switch. I give him a hug. This man too is grieving and can see that his heart is broken just being here. I thank him for organising the music, and he points at some CDs. 'Recordings of some of his songs,' he says gently. 'There is one for each of you and Shar, and your mom and dad, Li'. His voice is heavy with sadness.

My Mother is glaring, and so I walk to her to explain. Her face relaxes and she nods understandingly.

'But he's not staying, is he?'

I nod then too, her silent instruction received, and while I am uncomfortable about it, I know I must ask him to go.

He is bent, still organising the music and I touch him on the arm, saying quietly. 'Thanks so much for doing that, Dan, it really is appreciated.' I can hardly look him in the eye and so glance over to my family and my Brother. 'Sorry to have to ask but would you mind awfully giving us some privacy?'

His eyes flicker, and I read it that he is taken aback to be asked. 'Of course,' he says politely and retreats to the corner. He has not left yet, and so I look back to my family, some of whom are looking on, and others are standing quietly looking at the casket and my Sister-in-Law who is patting the cane work. I look back at my Brother's Sound Engineer Friend and do not say any more, hoping the stillness will be enough. Message silently received, he moves quietly out the side door into the courtyard out of sight.

Turning, I see my Husband step away from the Pillar who leaves the room. He explains that we need to start as there is another group expected shortly. We compose ourselves, ready to say farewell.

My Sister-in-Law is at the coffin and fidgeting with the handles of the casket, and my Father is soon at her side, placing his hand on hers to stem her action. She is genuinely shocked, frowns at him angrily and snatches her hand away from under his.

'I open,' she explains, determined.

'No, Li, we don't open,' my Father says gently.

'Yes!' she says, 'I say goodbye.' And more determined now starts to pull the bamboo stick that has been threaded through the latches along the length of the casket. My Father steps in and with a little more force has to grip her hand.

'No, Li. We can't. It is not good to see Ferg now,' he explains.

Tears well up in me as I witness my Sister-in-Law process agonisingly that she will not see her Husband again.

'I must see.' She is angry now. My Husband steps in to assist my Father. My Sister moves in to put her arm around my Brother's distraught wife.

'Li, he is not good. He too long in casket. Not healthy,' my Sister explains.

It is all become too much. My Sister-in-Law crumbles, bending at the knees as she lets out a wail. My Sister struggles to take the burden of the sudden weight. Her Husband and mine reach in to support her.

It is heart-breaking to watch. I feel angry and stupid that yet again we have failed my Brother's wife. To explain the sequence of events, not that we knew the micro detail ourselves, but at least to explain the significance of the closing of the lid when we were back in Schull. That it was the last time she would see his face, touch his body. Would she have lingered more then? Appreciated that last moment all the more? Now his body has started the slow decay, and it would not be pleasant for anyone's eyes.

My Sister stands stoic by my Sister-in law's side, holding her, supporting her as my Sister-in-Law's wail turns inwards to a quiet keening. I am devastated for her. For us. For us all.

I must ground myself. My Father had asked me to say the last few words. Having spent all of Sunday agonising over what to say, what to share, I feel it must be marked in a way my Brother would have chosen. I don't want to let them down. I do not wish to lose it mid-flow. I owe that to my Brother and my family.

I had racked my brain to dredge up memories significant of us all and what we had shared with my Brother over the years. Up until this point of post-funeral, pre-cremation, all the celebration of his life had been about Fergus the musician and friend, and I felt I wanted to capture a different part of him – the brother, the son, the husband. Researching, I flip through photos, letters, Facebook. But still, it does not feel right. Inexplicably, my own creative mind is not happy with this, so using my Brother's email and password, I spy on his most recent contacts by email. Who had he been in touch with, sharing what, working on what ideas? What had he been planning most recently?

In amongst the junk mail there is an email sent to a new acquaintance in the States. At first the name doesn't register, and then I remember my Brother explaining weeks before that he had been working on a commission for a new contact. Someone who had reached out to him through messenger on Facebook. Someone important, someone with connections. Opening up the mail, I see there is a short video attached. Feeling somewhat guilty at allowing myself the access, I go ahead and open the short clip.

The angle is shot from lap height as my Brother wheels towards some recent artwork that is clipped up on his filing cabinet by trouser-hangers to dry. The video is simple. Thirty seconds or so of a close-up of the work in progress, my Brother wheeling in close and back out again. There is no dialogue, but I can tell from the shifting hand and uneven driving that my Brother has been drinking. This does not come as a surprise, as he would sometimes take a few claiming it helped get creative juices flowing. Weighing up the cost of creativity against the suffering he would endure for days after.

I feel privileged to have this insight into a private moment. He alone, capturing his work while listening to some music. And that is when it hits me.

Too often my Brother is thought of as being totally caught up in his own music, but now I realise that unless he was working on a new piece or editing, he would never listen to his own compositions. Inspired by so many before him, he would listen to those that sparked his own creative juices. Those that spoke to him, made sense of his own living.

Moving my ear closer to the screen, I filter out all the background noise of his clicking and whirring wheelchair and concentrate on the music playing.

It is David Bowie.

Of course it is. Bowie's new album was released a few days before dying from liver cancer. *Black Star.* And instinctually I know this is what I will use.

My Brother was a huge Bowie fan and followed him closely over the years. He was deeply saddened to learn of Bowie's passing and naturally had downloaded the new album. Now, my Brother too is dead, and my own sadness feels somehow warm and settled in me.

Searching the lyrics on Google I am surprised to read what words my Brother was listening to and how appropriate they were now that he too has moved on. The lyrics are perfect. My gut tells me they are what I should share with my family. No one knows this story. It has not been shared before. I feel my Brother will forgive me, thank me even, for divulging this quiet private moment of his with the family as we prepare to say our last good-bye.

Something happened on the day he died,
Spirit rose a metre and stepped aside.
Someone else took his place, and bravely cried
I'm a black star, I'm a black star, I'm a black star.

I am crying reading the lyrics and at the idea of how my Brother too could also be the black star. I know this is perfect, yet I do not want to end my Brother's eulogy on a sad note. I must find something upbeat on which to end. Something ironic. Something that made my Brother happy.

Having previously scanned his emails, I take a moment to look a bit closer. There is a short mail there. The date and time confirm it was sent two days before his death. It is his last delivered email, sent from his iPhone.

Following a euphoric week of recording with his Oscar-Winning Friend and band, my Brother was on a high despite the deep grief he struggled with on losing his Music Friend. This email captures my Brother's feelings after the week of recording, focusing on the highs rather than the lows, as my Brother was wont to do. It was sent in reply to a thank-you email that had been sent by one of the Oscar Winner's band members after my Brother's hospitality and embrace. I feel it is a good way to conclude. Something that will be embedded gently in their memories.

I stand centre stage now, my Brother's casket in the corner of my eye, and focus on delivering these last few lines to those that hunger for some closure.

There is no rehearsal or replay here. Taking a breath, I give the backstory of how I found the two moments and then read the printouts in my hand. After sharing the David Bowies lyrics, I read my Brother's email response to my family gathered in front of me.

Sat, Jan 30, 2016 at 10:21pm

Dear —

I was in wonderland for the week. I don't know how long I have to live but I want to do this as often as possible or bearable for ye guys. I was absolutely over the moon and halfway round the Milky Way.

I wish I had thought of it back in 2003 but hey, dem's de breaks.

I feel so comfortable with you guys. I knew I would, but one could feel it was an all-round thing.

Also thrilled that the room situation seems to have been sonically pretty excellent.

Roll on next session which could be early March.

It's a funny thing about playing live and recording with some folks, there really is a bond develops [sic].

I love you too I can say unashamedly.

Until we meet or chat again I must say.....good Knight ☺ Hee Hee and Yahoo

ferg..

I call out the last 'Yahoo' with a false delight, trying to invoke his presence in the mail. Despite my faltering energy I am pleased with the reaction: sad smiles and slow appreciative nods. Stepping back into place amongst my family, I am hugged by my Husband and my Father. I stand aside to watch as one of the Pillars appears from the wings and moves into place to shut the panel doors. My Brother's final curtain.

My Brother's song plays now in the background, and we all stand shoulder to shoulder, arms interlocked, singing along with broken, croaking voices waiting for the panel doors to swing close.

In a moment of slapstick, one of the doors sticks and bounces in an effort to rotate on its hinges. The Pillar steps in to check the door's path and, pressing the button again, watches as the door struggles to close. *Is that you Ferg, having another joke – get us to laugh one final time?*

My Brother the joker. Not quite ready to go perhaps, or a sign that he is here with us.

Looking around me, I catch the eye of my Sister and she says as much out loud and we all laugh.

Lingering now, the Pillar finally fixes the door and when it clicks home there is an anti-climax.

The energy in the room changes and, as if after Mass, we filter towards the doors chatting quietly reliving the moment of the stuck door. My Brother's Music Friend is back in the room and dismantles the cables and speakers from the boom box. Already there are strangers waiting outside. It is business as usual at the city crematorium. Our turn is done. Over. Collect the ashes in ten days.

I register the next family arriving to say goodbye to their loved one. I smile the safe smile.

My Father tells us that we are booked for lunch in Bunnyconnellan's in Myrtleville, a short drive away. How lovely. It is a popular seafood eatery that sits up high on a precipice overlooking a cliff house that in turn overlooks the Celtic Sea. More importantly to me, we lived there once in the sleepy seaside village, and I associate one of my earliest memories with there.

I took my first steps in that same cliff house which my Parents had rented. One of my favourite home movie moments was captured there. Christmas Day many years ago, a time before disability or diagnosis for my Brother. My Brother cycles a new bike, my Sister pushes a new scooter while my Mother, with me in her arms, looks on. I am about two or three and dressed in just a jumper, wool tights and wellies and wriggling to be let down.

My Father works the camera and as usual has forgotten to turn on the sound. The camera scans across the movement of bike and scooter manned by my siblings when it comes round to me scampering down the hill, kicking off one boot, then the other. My Father sticks with my antics and soon the audience can witness my scampering momentum loosening my heavy cloth nappy in my tights, and in a moment nappy and tights too are abandoned. The camera pans out and in the frame you can see me delighted to be running amuck in my jumper and bare bottom as my Brother stops to point and laugh. My Sister, distracted, swerves and crashes headfirst into a nearby parked car.

It is all over in a moment as my Mother chases and swoops me up, me squirming in her arms as her head turns towards my crying Sister and then to the camera mouthing something angry at my Father.

The film turns black.

It is a moment etched into my mind. Not because it is a memory, as I am too young to remember it. But because it is a family moment caught in time. Caught on film. One that has been shown over the years with great commentary and laughter, at Christmases since, special birthdays, and family gatherings. A rite of passage enjoyed by each aspiring spouse.

Now as I stand on the same spot, I see the hill not so steep. The rented home is smaller, unoccupied, looking tired and dilapidated. The slipway has been battered by recent years' storms and the village shop is boarded up. Closed.

And yet I can play that scene over and over as we used to do at home. Playing the clip forwards and then backwards for greater comic effect. My striptease. My Brother pointing and laughing. My Sister's crash. My Sister's crash. My Brother pointing, laughing. My striptease. Now I play it forward and back again in my mind and slow it down. Pause it. My Brother pointing and laughing. Pointing and laughing. Laughing.

How life has come around to find us here again, this time without my Brother. I see his seven-year-old face, round and fresh looking, blond white hair, teeth too big for his mouth. Pointing and laughing at me. And I am grateful for the false memory. I share the memory now with my Sister-in-Law, try to explain the slide show that she would have witnessed time and again. She nods and smiles at me, but I can tell she does not remember which slide or image I am talking about. She does not know this memory. She does not share in it. Does she understand that this was a place of my Brother's before her time? Where he was a boy who used to run and play and poke sticks in the sand. I link her arm and point out the house and the slip, and we make our way down onto the beach. My girls join us; my Husband is already playing with my Son, building a sand dam on a small stream that splits the beach. The sea breeze blows about us, and soon we are besieged by two lumbering Great Danes who are enjoying the freedom off their leads, their owners following at a pace. My Sister-in-Law flinches as they bound by. I am a dog lover and cannot resist stretching out my arm as they pass. They delay a moment, and I pet and feel their beast energy and heat through their shiny grey coats, their firm muscles and soft warmth. My Sister-in-Law, ever wary of dogs, stands back. The hounds do not stand still and are off again to run and jump and play, their owners apologising as they jog passed.

The beach is no longer ours alone, the moment has ceased. We make our way up the slip, back towards the cars.

The film has turned black again.

My Sister-in-Law announces that she will go to Kinsale to link up with a Chinese friend who lives there. She will not go back to Schull. Family glances bounce briefly from one to another. There is a discussion about who she will travel with. I offer to take her.

My Sister-in-Law's announcement is not a surprise. There is no knowing what way she will jump. I don't think any of us, including herself, were prepared to have her go back to West Cork, to an empty house.

We had not thought that far ahead.

None of us have any idea what the next few days will bring. My Husband and Sister's Husband must return to work. The children to school. I am not ready to show up for work myself, happy to greet time as it passes. My Parents will return to Schull. My Sister will go home with her family. We are all going our separate ways. A detour is not an issue for me. Nor is having the company of my Sister-in-Law for the hour or so it will take to get there.

I am willing to spend a few hours in the car mindful of her needs. I discover my Daughters and Son have chosen to drive with their Father, and I am left to bring my Sister-in-Law to Kinsale on my own. I accept this, as the conversation can be dictated by her. I am ashamed to register that I have never spent more than thirty minutes alone with her. This will be my longest with just her company. I owe it to her, to my Brother, to give her at least the car journey.

Mindful of not letting the Secret slip.

We move off in convoy, me following my Husband's car as the rest break into different routes, homeward bound.

My Sister-in-Law has my full attention now as she talks animatedly about my Brother. How much he loved me. She has a knack. It is a Chinese way. To charm and compliment. Talk up your good points. How my Brother trusted me, respected me. Then she compares me to my Sister, how I am better than her. At least that is what I hear at first and then realise that no, her words are carefully chosen. She is talking up the skills that I have that my Sister does not. There is a difference. They spent three weeks in each other's company in China on that family trip. When she was alone with my Sister, did my Sister-in-Law do the same with her? Did she talk up my Sister's skills that I do not have when it is just the two of them. Two sides to a coin. Two faces. In any case she has my full attention and then her talk turns to her own relationship with my Brother. How he had taught her so much, to love, to be loved, to love herself. In private detail she describes their love life, how in earlier days he would make love to her, and then when he was no longer as able, how he taught her to love herself.

I feel awkward and embarrassed at the matter-of-fact detail that she shares. I am grateful for her broken English as I don't fully understand or catch what she is telling me. While she may be getting some solace in the sharing, I get mine from the fact that the physical detail is lost in her dense accent.

I respectfully nod and make listening noises as she talks.

On arriving to Kinsale, she is soon on the phone and making arrangements with her Chinese friend. I find my Husband's car that is parked nearby, and my Eldest joins me now for the homeward leg. We are to drive home in convoy and leave my Sister-in-Law to seek solace amongst her own.

TUESDAY

February 9

It is a week since my Brother's death. And it is as if a whole lifetime has passed us by. His house is still now. Sits in the dark as if holding its breath. My Brother's wife is still away. Flitting from one friend to another. She has told my Father she will go back to China to her own family in the next few days and will return briefly to West Cork before she departs.

Late as it may well be, I search on Google for Chinese traditions around death and the many customs that form part of that ancient, vast culture. Then I spy something significant about the seventh day.

I read that it is believed by some that on this day the spirit of the dead wanders in search of their home, and so to help guide them, the family drape the front door with red sashes and banners with the spirit's name to help in case of disorientation. Rice is scattered at the doorway so that their footprints will be revealed should they cross the threshold, and lanterns light the way to help guide them.

As much for myself as for my Sister-in-Law, I decide to re-enact this and go about duplicating what I can, using materials and candles that I have to hand at my Mother's and Brother's house.

Instead of banners, I make a poster of my Brother's band name, using red letters on a white card and place it low enough so that his drifting spirit, perhaps out of habit, might be at wheel chair height. I scatter the uncooked rice at the threshold and place candles in storm lanterns and nightlights in jam jars. A gifted glass butterfly sits amongst them by the door. It is a simple set-up but one I am pleased to have completed in good timing within the seventh day.

I take a photo and send it to my Step-Nephew and his mother.

It is perhaps a late gesture acknowledging their culture, but if nothing else it might be appreciated. In any case, I feel the better for having done it.

Dreams come and go.

In some, my Brother is walking, skinny and with his waddle, but still walking. Healthy. In others he is already dead, and the dream is focused on the living and the sadness. Most are sad, few are happy. And then there is the one from last night. Where I dreamed it is that moment when the paramedics have dragged him from his bed to the floor and they are pounding on his chest but not quite doing enough, not giving him air. I stand witness, useless, feeling frustrated, desperate. And then his eyelids flutter and he is breathing again and his eyes open, flashes of blue looking about, trying to focus. Frightened. It is just us now, and instantly I am on my knees on the floor by his side. I take him by the hand and cup his fingers. It is our sibling hold. As if I am his child sister again and my hand is too small and I wrap my fingers crescent moon-like into his. It is just the fingertips that curve into each other, but it is secure and safe and lovely. I take his hand gently and bend my head towards him slowly so not to frighten him.

'Hey Ferg.'

His stellar eyes find mine and there is a weak loving smile, and I feel the heat of relief spread through me. He is alive, just. And then his face softens and his focus deepens. I feel a shift. I sense he is asking me something without asking it, and a wave of sadness washes over me.

No! I know what he wants but I do not want what he wants. I won't speak it. My sadness turns to selfish want but my love for him pushes it aside. This is not about what I need. I scan his unfurrowed loving face and my tears are brimming because I know what is coming. That dull ache rises from my stomach. I grip his hand a bit tighter and place the other gently on his shoulder. My eyes find his again.

'It's time isn't it?' I quietly ask.

He smiles again, eyes softening 'Yes, Lyd.' And he nods his head on the hard floor. I nod too, holding my breath and struggle to hold back my tears as he smiles for me one last time. His eyes, loosing grip on mine, close shut. He slips away.

It is a dream of course. And I awake with real tears flowing. Big fat gushing tears. I am alone in the bed and let them come now, sobbing because he is not here with me. He is not here at all. My Brother is gone. He is really gone.

Oh, gosh, how I loved you so.

It WAS time.

As hard as it is to say goodbye.

No matter the hows, or the whys or the wherefores.

It was your time to go.

And sure, haven't you just told me so?

AUGUST 2016

Six months in. I am slowly adjusting to the vacuum my Brother has left when the In-Laws arrive.

No doubt the intention is genuine and sincere. But my angry cloud is growing, and lumps of nimbuses stuff my head. A cumulonimbus mass pushes up against my rib cage; slate grey with patches of black.

The dark side of me conjures up a sense of visitors ticking a box in the 'how to support the grieving' checklist. See for themselves how we are coping. As if it is the right thing to do. And so it must be done.

My various In-Laws have planned their visits separately, albeit over a period of three consecutive weekends during peak summer. They arrive in August, when the summer season in West Cork is at its height, and we are besieged by *yachties* who bring their airs of entitlement, first world problems and bulging wallets.

I feel anxious and resentful about their coming.

Now I must relive stories and emotions once more. Because of reasoning and education, I understand that this is a process I need to go through. My Brother is dead and will remain so regardless of any other's endeavours. My own life will continue.

I convince myself to accept the process.

THE PARENTS-IN-LAW

Our own Little House does not have the space to accommodate their needs and I am unwilling to give up our marital bed. With my own Mother and Father away, an invitation is extended to my Husband's parents to stay at the Big House in Schull. Friday evening, my Husband settles them into the house west along, with a promise of joining them for breakfast the next day. They have an evening for themselves. On

Saturday, it is decided, for ease of hosting and company, that we too will move out west, masking the move as a mini-staycation.

I must don my Daughter-in-Law mask. But I am not ready for the family stage this time. I feel trouble brewing and am gearing up for pre-emptive tactics. I cannot explain it other than that I would prefer to be at home alone, *circling the wagons*, planning a weekend with my Husband. Not having to bring up social graces and niceties with those outside my circle. I remind myself they are my Husband's kin. He endures mine almost daily, having moved to West Cork over twenty years ago. It is a novelty for his family to make the trip south: "It's so far away." He loves them and really I do too. And so, I dust off the mask.

Our first social engagement is breakfast. The War Room is once more put to use, to a breakfast setting that it is hoped will meet their expectations, and my Husband and I wait for them at the small round table.

His Mother, as always, arrives first. In her pearls, slacks and twin-set and self-coiffed short white hair, she looks younger than her 70 years. I imagine this is how Grace Kelly might have looked had she reached a similar age. Respectful morning air kisses are exchanged.

We determine the quality of last night's sleep and the comfort of the bed while tea is poured. Excuses are offered, as always, for my Father-in-Law, who will arrive down a bit later (he likes to take his time to complete his daily ablutions and grooming). I am already inexcusably irritated.

'So how are you coping?' my Mother-in-Law asks me, while she milks her tea.

'Oh, I am okay. Up and down really. Some days are better than others.'

'I suppose all you are looking for is sympathy,' she says, buttering her soda bread.

My cumulonimbus slams within my chest, winding me. 'Excuse me?' I growl.

'Mom!' My Husband glares at his mother.

A searing heat rises up through my throat and flashfloods my brain. I push at my cloud to try and stem any thundering outburst. What was it I learned about confrontation? Respond, do not react.

'Did I hear you correctly?' I ask. I look at my Husband's blanched face. 'Sympathy? You think I am looking for sympathy?'

'She didn't mean it that way,' my Husband says, floundering. His mother looks from her son to me and back again, looking confused and uncertain at what she has said and why it caused such a reaction. In a year or so we would understand that forgetfulness and malapropisms were becoming more frequent – but now the lip-slip is taken as a slight, and all I feel is anger at the woman looking at me blankly.

Fearful of saying something that I might regret later, I rise to standing, forcing my chair back, and stride from the room, my Husband's petitions falling on closed ears.

The noise of the TV diverts me to the sitting-room, and I find solace in the innocent, calm space occupied by my Son. I sit in close, squeeze him to me, kiss his head. He hugs me back, eyes not moving away from the screen.

Sympathy! Hah! I mull over it. No, sympathy is not what I am looking for. Not what I need. Not wanted. I do not want anyone's sadness or sad looks. They can keep it.

But what *do* I want? If not sympathy, what am I looking for? What do I need?

I want my Brother back. That is what I want. But then, what good is that? Him in the state that he had become.

In a fictional world, I would have a younger version. The one that could walk and run and tease and mock. A genetically perfect version.

One that, as a youth could have picked me up and swung me around like a 'real' big brother. One that would have raced me across fields and won, would have climbed trees and climbed them higher. Swam with me and swam faster. Delivered dead arms and punches and left bruises. One that would have been the full-bodied son to my Father – an all-action, hunting, shooting, fishing sort of boy, instead of me consciously compensating as one in his stead with my tomboy antics and laddish behaviour.

But any physical Brother that might have been was long before. Before he was 10 and his legs started to get heavy; before the postman commented on his 'funny walk'; before the local GP referred him to a specialist; before London for needles and tests and life-changing news of muscle deterioration and a creeping disability. Before my Mother was delivered the chilling (inaccurate) prognosis by a finger clicking medicine man: "In a wheelchair by 12 and at 18...." Finger snap.

By his mid-teens, my Brother no longer had the capacity to be as physical as a big brother should. Any physical big brother is a fictional one. The brother I would have back again would be obese and depressed and unable. The most recent one, brain smog-filled and body defunct. My Brother had become miserable. I would not have that back. To have him back would be for myself, not for him.

No, I do not seek sympathy. Nor do I want my Brother back. Not really. Fate intervened. Perhaps Faith. In any case it was out of our hands.

And I am grateful to my Mother-in-Law for helping me realise and accept this. In that moment I remain irritated, but on the whole, I am grateful for her words and for lifting the veil of smog that had snuck in around my own head.

In anticipation of the next batch of visitors, a big food-shop needs to be done. Since my Brother's death, I have become a recluse and am settled into a hermit status a bit too comfortably. As a result, I have depleted our dry store of pasta, beans and rice. I draw a line at having to become creative with the tinned sardines and dried lentils. Once my weekly chore, shopping of late has become daily short trips to the local petrol station for eggs and bread and milk and frozen creations to ensure the family do not starve. Food is of no interest to me (despite six months of continuously grazing), only I know I must feed the masses and need to bring a healthier routine back into my life. An impromptu food list comes to mind: dog food, cat food, meat for dinners. And wine. Priorities.

I have procrastinated enough, and my hotelier Husband sacrifices a precious free Saturday and commits to doing a big one on the condition that I come along, for the change of scene. "It will be good for you to get out," he says.

We head to the nearest German superstore, my Husband taking the lead and pushing the trolley, with me moping in tow. He talks up fruit and seasonal vegetables and cuts of meat, suggesting the menu for the week ahead. I visualise the food and effort needed to cook it and sigh at the thought. I am exhausted already, and we have not yet completed the first aisle.

My bones are heavy, legs weighted. Head dull. I feel like I am sludging through an invisible mire of molasses. I take great relief in not recognising any of the faces that walk the aisles, relinquishing any responsibility for donning my social mask to greet and engage.

And then I spot a Local. A familiar face. She is true blood. Old blood. Not a blow-in like us. An air of entitlement encompasses her. Seeing her brings up flash memories of when I was a child and on our annual sailing holidays, moored off the Schull harbour wall, and then gifted the freedom of rural village life, aged 10 or so, often let off to my own devices, drawn as always to the hill-top play-ground where I would vie with her over swing sets and 'king-of-the-castle' at the top of the ten-foot slide.

And I am a child once more and feel as if we are back in the playground and herself domineering the yard. Despite many years passing, and life getting in our way, that old feeling of flight or fight (for we each did both) surfaces in me and my eye seeks a quick exit. Somehow, I manage to politely greet her in passing. I sludge by.

A little later, my Husband and I get to the till and the chore of bag-filling is looming ahead of me. I am nonplussed.

'It's ok,' my Husband says. 'I'll do it.'

He chats away with the till attendant, and I slowly make my way outside, trying to remember where we parked the car. Standing for a moment, I scan the car park and, turning on the spot, see the Local approaching me. A cold sweat crawls up my back. I dread to think what she feels she has to say.

'I'm sorry, Lydia, but you look so miserable,' she says, still walking towards me, 'I thought you could do with a hug.'

I am blindsided, and before I know it, she has me embraced. Her hug is genuine and warm and lovely. Her voice is soft in my ear, 'I know it has been a very tough time for you all.'

Tears well. Releasing the hug, I mumble, 'Thank you.'

Saying no more, she squeezes my hand, turns and walks away, leaving me behind in an eddy of compassion and unexpectedness. Swirling in my own penitence.

THE HUSBAND'S BROTHER AND FAMILY

My Son is very excited to have his young cousins stay. I am less enthusiastic. It is the first time I will see my Husband's Sister-in-Law since before her conspicuous absence at my Brother's funeral.

My Husband and his Brother are good friends now. There was a time when they were not. The have put years of sibling rivalry and bullying behind them. My Husband's Brother, the eldest son, took his place in the family very seriously and made sure his younger siblings understood this. Years of torment and shoving and teasing and entitlement. It took the two older boys to be men, and a time of emigration to the UK, to relinquish any grudges.

When my Husband was still my boyfriend, we decided to take six months to Euro-rail as an excuse to live together. The plan was to make a short stop to visit his brother near London. A year and a half later we were still there – the British and easy renting offering us a life with jobs and togetherness with no judging eyes.

I remember a Bromley basement sitting room cramped with airs and graces and quality wines, where our gourmand hosts, my Husband's Brother and his Scottish girlfriend, educated us on Hungarian Bull's Blood and twenty-eight-day-hung steaks. As usual, my Husband's Brother was holding court and getting irritated at his younger brother's opinion. I don't recall the topic, but I can clearly see my Husband's Brother red-faced and frazzled at the viewpoint offered by my Husband. Mulling over and at the same time appearing confused about what new information my Husband had to share. Struggling with not wanting to listen to his younger sibling yet still be being curious to hear more. Just not from him.

'Shut the fuck up.' And then, wrinkling his nose, 'What are you saying?'

And in my mind's eye I can see my Husband attempting to begin again and his Brother interrupting once more, 'Shut the fuck up', brandishing his cigar and then leaning in once more, 'What are you saying?'

My Husband sitting up and saying, 'Which do you want?'

His Brother, pulling a face, 'What?'

'Do you want me to shut the fuck up or explain a bit more?'

It is comical and I start to giggle. My Husband starts up too, jokingly repeating what his brother has said.

It is like a switch has gone on in my Husband's Brother's head as he stalls and reboots.

'You mightn't like my opinion,' my Husband adds. 'You don't even have to agree with it. But it is *my* opinion and I am entitled to it. Now do you want me to shut the fuck up or do you want me to continue?'

My Husband's Brother then starts to laugh too and gives his brother a light-fisted dead arm. It is a breaking point. A line drawn in the sand. *Brothers-in-arms.*

My Husband's Sister-in-Law is a force of nature in character and determination – admittedly, a bit like myself, the Little men appearing to have similar taste in strong-minded and opinionated women. She and I are both children of the 70s with similar taste in music and movies and an empathy for the struggle of motherhood. The big difference being height, and size and, due to her bones failing her, daily pain management. She is the taller of us both by at least six inches. Her temper is the only thing short about her.

It hurt that she had not attended my Brother's funeral and, six months later, I am still not quite over that snub.

Too many families would use such a slight to allow an offence to fester. On my Father's side, there are cousins who have not spoken for years, the original reason unclear to the younger generation. Urban myths circulate my Father's home village about wives falling out with each other over their respective husbands' actions, the husbands having forgiven each other within days, the wives carrying the vehemence and vengeance for decades.

If I don't let this slight go, this too might fester, wedge a gap between families. It might be forty years hence and grandchildren might ask what the feud was all about, and I might give a warped answer. Now, I must face my inner demon, allow the family visit and hope there is some give and take where we all are satisfied with the outcome.

My Husband is a witness to the surprise apology. It is given in our farmhouse kitchen as I stand at the Belfast sink, hands submerged in suds and dirty water, looking out the window as the birds perform acrobats on the bird feeder. The admission is given to my back.

'Lydia, I am sorry I didn't make Fergus's funeral. I should have been there.'

And there it is. It is out. And I am so grateful it has been said behind me, so I can take a moment to release the rush of blood, unclench my jaw.

Turning slightly, I side-glance at my Husband who has taken to carving sections from the table candle with a bread knife. A quick eye cast in my direction, my Husband a silent witness.

'Thank you for saying that,' I say, pausing mid-rinse, unable to turn to face her just yet.

She fills the gap, mumbling excuses of prior commitment and expense, and in my head I am thinking, 'Stop talking', but the words keep coming and excuses are running thinner and I still can't look at her. And then I realise I must look at her to make her stop.

I am saved by the sound of a car beeping.

'Oh, here is Mom and Dad,' I say and, with perfect timing, my Mother calls out the familiar 'Hello-o' as she pushes in the front door.

Polite greetings are made, and I have the excuse of engaging in pleasantries while fresh coffee is brewed. My cloud pales and dissipates within me.

Initial greeting completed, my Parents chit-chat with the visitors and my Husband's Sister-in-Law uses the gifted time-out to make an excuse and disappears upstairs.

And I replay the gifted apology in my head.

Over the years I have never heard my Husband's Sister-in-Law say sorry.

I might surmise the issue stems from her younger life when she and her younger brother engaged in a constant battle of wills. I believe the two have yet to share their 'Shut the fuck up' moment.

When it comes to apologies, my Husband's Sister-in-Law, will skirt around an issue and resort to performing circus acts to avoid having to say the humble words, 'I'm sorry.'

But today I have been gifted these words. With sincerity. I am still whirling from having heard them spoken from her lips.

Coming back down the stairs again, my Husband's Sister-in-Law descends into a conversation that is in full flow and finds a space at the kitchen counter, leaning against it. Purposely, I walk close to her and flank her hip, deliberately leaning against the counter too. We are silent, heat pulsating between us. The space uncomfortably close.

My Mother is engaged in a story and, while all eyes are on her, I turn to my Husband's Sister-in-Law and gently nudge her hip with my elbow. I turn and look up at her, so that I can catch her eye. 'Thanks for that earlier,' I whisper. 'It means a lot.'

Smiling, she throws her arm around my shoulders and squeezes me into her, fluffing up my cloud like you would a cushion on a chaise longue. I am thinking she is as satisfied as me and we are both the lighter for it. Cloud-stepping. Friends again.

MY HUSBAND'S SISTER

She comes alone. A solo mission. A mission with purpose.

The eldest of my Husband's siblings – their mother having had six children in nine years – my Husband's Sister mimicked her own mother in dress and hair and mothering when she was young. Never having offspring of her own, this firstborn's instinct is to mind instead her siblings and any children they have.

She was abroad when my Brother died – the other side of the world with work – and she made it very clear at the time that she was devastated that she couldn't make it back in time for the funeral. My Husband, following that long-distance phone call, reported tears, sincere apologies and lots of guilt felt on her part.

Her arrival now brings with her Dublin dust and stiff joints, and following hugs and toilet and kettle on, we soon cover courtesy questions of how my Parents and my Sister are faring. Her coat is still warm when she asks, 'How is Li?'

A flash storm floods my mind. A surge of anger inflamed. Thoughts of my Sister-in-Law's past confession that when my Brother would die, she would return to China and her family and investments there. I cannot share any resentment at her escaping the funeral aftermath. Escaping responsibility and avoiding friends/family-in-need here. I do not mention the anger at being left to pick up the pieces. My despair at her leaving the business of his hand-typed will and her widow's pension and sorting my Brother's business to me and my Father. I do not reveal the utter sadness at having to be her administrator at my Brother's computer. To sort his estate and royalties, all the while staring at their personal effects and his ghost and last moments echoing in my ears. I do not mention my disappointment in my Brother for not planning for the inevitable, for his failing in his responsibilities as a husband, for not ensuring his diabetic wife was set up with health insurance, a pension, a future. For not settling his affairs.

Instead, I update my Husband's Sister with my Brother's Wife having returned to China with excuses about her 85-year-old father still living there. To be close to clan and kin. And the Chinese way of grieving.

And then I move onto the storytelling. The telling, the story. Six months in and I am easier with the recounting. I have retold the week of my Brother's death so often in person, in my head and on my keyboard. So I tell it as it was, staying brave and tearless. The days before where he grieved for his Music Friend, his Death Day, the Wake, the Celebration, the After-party, the Cremation. Our Little House kitchen witnessing another in-law moment. I tell it as would a seanchaí. Like the folk of old who sat at firesides and would recount and relive and embody. I tell it so that in time my story has become her story and a part of her can conjure up false memories, as if she too had been there for it all. She wells, tears fall, and apologies for her absence are made yet again. She sniffles and snorts. The kitchen table weighs heavy with elbows and coffee and grief and snot-filled kitchen paper.

Pausing, offering a brief moment to recover, I restart. This time focusing on the yet to come, the good, the approaching anniversary concerts, the update on the documentary and the fundraising and album in the making and the intended scattering of ashes and moving on. Turning the sadness into life – the new celebrations, the practical. The new normal.

We are smiling again, looking forward. Tea is slurped and biscuits shared.

But I do not speak of the Secret. That is kept yet. Kept still and silent and quiet in my chest. Caged behind my ribs for safe keeping. For now.

OVERLOAD

Wednesday morning, February 3

The morning after my Brother's death, my Father asks me if I have the codes and passwords to his computer. I do. It is on the other side of the sheet where I wrote his funeral plans back in July.

We go to my Brother's house and it is devoid of its usual energy of music and noise and living. My Sister-in-Law has not yet arrived into the country, and we are ensconced in my Brother's house rifling through his business drawers and files. For what I don't know. We will certainly not find him there.

Instinctively I go to my Brother's Mac and see there is no power there. As a PC user myself, I lack confidence to understand what I am doing wrong and so seek a power button or light as the source of getting it switched on. I step towards his other computer, the 'big MAC' , the one he uses for recording his music and realise I don't know how to switch that on either.

'How do I turn this on?' I call out to my Daughter, who has come down with us to the house. She looks over my shoulder and gently but deliberately pushing me aside, leans in to examine the screen more closely. I check the sockets and notice there is no red power light in the surge cord as would normally display on my own. My Father's attention is now called as my Daughter asks if he knows how to turn it on. He is a Mac user and so might have a better idea. I drift out of the room; there are too many of us all staring at the screen, and my own ignorance is not helping the situation. I am already exhausted by it.

Wandering into the main room and on into my Brother's bedroom, I sit on his bed. Shifting my gaze absently towards the window, my eye is drawn outside to a leaf of wagging ivy. Might it be my Brother waving in at me?

I hear my Daughter call out something about electricity. I know from her voice that she has moved from the conservatory and is somewhere out in the hall and then says more clearly, 'Should this switch be down?'

I am guessing she is looking at the fuse board. I am not really listening and let my mind be still and numb and try to sense my Brother, wondering again where his spirit has gone.

My Father makes his way out and I hear him say something to my Daughter and I have stood now, curious to know more, and am making my way around my Brother's medical bed when, in that same movement, there is deafening cacophony of sound and air.

My Brother's bed resurrected pushes up air, and his mattress swells twofold raising upwards, and this is synchronised with his oxygen mask as it leaps from sleeping position into a snake-like dance screaming for air like a venting banshee. I shout with the sheer fright of it all and my Sister, who had been standing at the opening to the kitchen, screams in fright with me.

And then I register a new terror. The absolute horror of reality hits me like a freight train and I hear my Sister plead, 'Oh Jesus Christ.'

I feel a tide of wretchedness crawl up from deep within. Running around the bed, I cannot turn off the hissing mask and pulsating bed fast enough. I can't speak for the desperation to quieten it, my voice has failed me. Silencing the machines, I collapse onto his bed. Suck up the reality of it. My Brother did not die by the hand of God nor because his body had failed him.

I crumble at the waist, head bent into my hands, and erupt. What comes out is a low long pitiful wail. My Daughter has appeared at my side, bent into me. Silently cradling. Only for the bed under me and her arms wrapped round me, I would be on the floor.

'What? Jesus Fucking Christ, what?' My Father has run into the room trying to understand what has happened, his face pinched in pain and confusion.

I cannot answer him and turn away, bent into my Daughter dry-retching my wails. All I can hear beyond my own noise is my Sister declaring desperately: 'Oh my sweet God, we killed him, we killed him.'

'No one must know,' my Father commands.

All three of us are stood limply in front of him. My Sister, my Daughter, and me.

'We can't tell your Mother. Or Li,' he says. We nod. 'It will kill them.'

A storm cloud has lodged in my chest cavity. Dark grey, ominous. Sinister.

My mind's eye conjures up an image of my Brother and the horror he must have experienced in that moment – when the switch tripped and both air and bed failed him. I dispel the image – bring my attention to the here...the now...my Father's face. Ashen green. Sharpened furrows cut into his brow. I can't look at my Sister. Nor my Daughter. Fat tears are still flowing down my face and I wipe them away with the heel of my hand.

'What could have tripped it?' my Father asks no one in particular.

None of us has an answer.

'Jesus Christ,' my Father says, wiping his face.

'Why didn't the generator kick in?' my Daughter asks.

'It has to be manually started,' my Sister explains quietly. 'Maybe it was the paramedics?' she adds, 'some of their equipment?'

'I dunno,' my Father says.

None of us do.

And there is that image again in my head.

On his last morning, my Brother alive, preparing for his day ahead. Due to go to Schull hospital respite for the rest of the week. A semi-holiday for him. He loved the nurses, the bed, and the food there. 'Like a five-star hotel,' he liked to joke. 'Where they'll even wash my bollox.'

His morning spent making phone calls to friends, to the hospital, to us. Utilising an excited burst of energy to plan, to organise. The timing of his calls now making sense. Having rung my Mother, members of the family, his Home Help. And that fatal decision to stay in bed to do his nebuliser.

'Maybe it was his nebuliser?' I suggest. 'Maybe that did something? His bed was on, his air, did the liquid trip it or something?'

My Father frowns. 'That doesn't make sense.' He shakes his head. 'Jesus Christ,' he says again.

The utter sadness of it.

My Brother's face comes to mind. Him struggling to breathe. What those ten, twenty, thirty seconds must have been like. The terror for him. The helplessness. The cancelled phone calls. The emergency number. What did he say? What was he able to get out to them between snatched breaths? Did he lose consciousness while on to them? Their unanswered returned calls. Does that explain the gap? The pain of it. Emotionally, physically. What went through his mind? The loneliness of it. Alone. The final moment as his mind left this world and slipped away from us. Did he fade feeling a gentle pull or was it an agonising fight to try and suck something, anything, into the last of his one working lung? My sweet, sweet Brother.

Fresh tears flow and I turn away to face his bedroom and all the equipment that failed him. 'All because of a FUCKING tripped switch,' I say aloud. My sadness is replaced with anger. 'Aggghhh. FOR FUCK SAKE,' I scream out to the room. To my Brother. I feel a huge sense of failure. Guilt. The guilt of it. No one here to assist. In that briefest of moments.

'Christ. If he had gotten up like he was supposed to have he could have done his fucking nebuliser sitting up. Then the tripped switch wouldn't have mattered,' I reasoned, crying angrily.

My Sister steps into me and embraces me, both of us crying, heaving now.

'He would have been able to breathe on his own sitting up,' I blubber, my nose full of snot and I can't see through my own tears. My Sister rubs my back and squeezes me quiet. There is nothing she can say. She can't speak for her own tears.

I push out of her embrace, back into the now. My Father has sat desolately on the arm rest of the couch. My Daughter stands stoically alone, a bystander, a witness, her own face mirroring a new grief that has enveloped us.

Later, I walk into my Brother's house. Everybody else is up at the main house, my Husband in the village making plans. My Sister, my Father and my Daughter have all retreated into shadowed corners. Quiet. I give the excuse to my Mother of wanting to give my Brother's house a final once-over in anticipation of the arrival of my Sister-in-Law later.

I am really looking for answers.

Walking from my Brother's hall into the main room, I notice a small bundle of clothes that are left on the arm of the chair that sits on the bottom of the stairs. Unfolded, creased and cold to touch, they have the look of a pile that has been temporarily plonked there by someone, expecting to come back to them and fold them any moment now. But that someone never did. It is a small enough bundle of a couple of socks, t-shirt, bed sheet. My Brother's. They are hovering, almost suspended in a frozen moment. A nudge in any direction would topple them onto the seat of the chair or onto the floor. In any case they are sat there all the while waiting to be put away. I pair the socks and roughly fold the t-shirt my Brother would never wear again. I raise it to my nose and suck in its smell. His is there, but it is faint, overpowered by washing detergent and something else. What is that? Tumble-dried air? The fitted bed sheet is more complicated to fold; in my thirty or so years of bed making and linen folding, I have yet to master a fitted sheet. While I did not care too much about the creases, I knew my Mother would not appreciate a roll fold as opposed to matching the bends and the corners.

Struggling with what corner goes where, a niggling thought takes up in my head and it stops me in motion. *Tumble-dried air*. Stepping back into the hall, I open the large pine folding doors that hide the stacked washing machine and dryer and stare at them now.

The dryer is empty. Door unlocked and ajar. Turning the knob to twenty, I close the door and wait. A scraping, dragging noise sounds from behind the drum and then a deep dark smell of burning rubber assails me. I stand staring at the machine. My eyes follow the line of sight to the fuse board and back to the machine again. The scraping noise piercing my eardrum, the burning smell turning my stomach. My heart quickens. I grab at the dryer door, reefing it open, putting an instant stop to its screeching. Turning my back on the machine, I snatch the folded bundle and scurry into my Brother's room, cram the t-shirt and socks home into his clothes press, run upstairs to the hot press and shove the sheet in amongst the others roughly stacked there. My heart is pounding against my chest, my head running through all the possibilities. My Brother, his bed, his oxygen, his nebuliser, all the stupid plugs, the extension leads, his sound system, his computers, this house, the wiring system – and the screaming tumble dryer. All being run on a twenty-something-year-old circuit system.

Is that why my Sister-in-Law used clothes horses all this time? Set up throughout the conservatory, draped with damp sheets and knickers, socks and t-shirts. My Mother complaining to my Brother how awful it looked. All that damp in the air not being good for his lungs.

'I like it,' he had said. 'Gives a homely look about the place.'

There is no way of testing the load now. There is no way of repeating the sequence. His oxygen, his bed, his nebuliser, his TV, the dryer. I am not an electrician but even I understand that a circuit has its limits. It might carry four machines, but could it carry a faulty fifth? Was that what proved too much for the circuit system? Causing it to overload? Trip the switch? Switch the trip. Sending my Brother on a new journey.

I hurry back to the hall. The smell lingers. I am terrified that someone will come and ask questions. Questions I do not want to answer. Connect the dots. Opening the front door, I waft it back and forth.

Dissipate the smell. Releasing the weight of it.
Imagining my Brother's soul running with it.
His particles taken up by a south westerly.
Upward dancing now
Then drifting
Soaring through the upper atmosphere
Atoms lifted by the solar wind
Interstellar
Free to form his own molecular cloud
Somewhere in that *space that lies*
Between a joke and a smile
And beachcomb(s) the empty mile.

Prayer before a Voyage

Be my weather,
Blow thru me like the wind.
Wind in invisible shapes about my ribs,
Rain on me,
Be my winter.

For what do I wish?
Not for stone, nor for wood,
Nor of water nor of flesh,
But to meet you in the space that lies
Between a joke and a smile
And beachcomb the empty mile
Be my weather,

Blow through me like the wind.
Wind invisible shapes about my ribs,
Rain on me,
Be my winter.

FIRST ANNIVERSARY

Thursday, February 2, 2017

I am parked on the Bridge of Woe, engine ticking over while my Daughter runs into the main house to collect a framed painting by my Brother. It will be donated as an incentive to entice contributions for a social media crowd fundraiser (to complete the documentary movie) that will be launched this evening. There are high hopes of bringing the completed feature to Sundance and Cannes.

My Son sits in the car with me, and I look over towards my Brother's house. It is no longer visible. The house remains; it is just on the other side of an eight-foot wall. All part of a greater plan. One that was mapped out before my Brother's death. To split the properties in anticipation of putting one or both houses on the market. It took great persuasion to convince my Mother to leave a stile in the wall for easy access between the two worlds. So it would allow us all to flit from one house to the other. We can close it again when a sale comes through.

To see the divide in reality is disquieting. I have taken to calling it the Great Wall. Separating East from West. My Mother has softened it with a natural stone and cement render, climbing plants and planted bedding. It is still a big wall. The Great Wall a metaphoric symbol of the bureaucracy blockers that we have had to endure.

Since my Brother's death, my Father and I have been executing my Brother's will. Finalising papers, transferring his royalties, bank accounts. Arranging it all to be signed over to my Sister-in-Law. His Widow. My Sister-in-Law, being away in China, has made the process all the more difficult. I have learned that in Chinese culture the chief mourner gets a year to grieve. To process. They do not talk of money. Of Wills. Of inheritance. My Sister-in-Law tells me that the Chinese do not believe in Wills. To talk of them is bad luck. Bad chi.

Yet man cannot live on bread alone. Or on my Father. To strike a balance has been difficult. Western laws require signatures, notarised death certificates, witnessed wills. A lot of time. Patience. Lots and lots of patience. It has been a long, messy and frustrating process. There have been days when I want to pound the keyboard of my Brother's computer when administrating on his widow's behalf. Instead, I scream at the screen.

I stare at the Great Wall while the car air-conditioning blows warm, thinking of a Sony conference call to the US that needs to be made. Allow for Pacific Standard Time. I look down at the clock. It is 12:32.

My stomach plummets.

#Fergendipity.

This exact moment twelve months before my Brother dialled 999. It was the beginning of his end. Tears well up. The Secret remains. More have been told. Now you know too. I relive the agony for him in my mind. How long is a minute?

'Are you okay, Mom?' my Son asks.

I nod, swiping away the tears that slide on my cheek. 'Yeah.'

'You thinking about Uncle Ferg?'

I nod again. Keep facing forward.

He unbuckles his belt, leans in between the front seats. Rubs my shoulder.

Tender thoughts are broken with the car door being yanked open and my Daughter jumps in with the painting. I feel her looking at me.

'What's up?' she asks curiously.

I tap at the car clock. Not wanting to vocalise it.

'Oh. Is it Ferg time?' she mumbles. The Secret hangs around her too.

I nod, putting the car into gear and head east towards Ballydehob.

I can't help but follow the clock count as I drive. Another minute. Another. And another. Eight minutes in. The time I figure it really took for my Brother to pass from this world. Eight minutes. Longer till the ambulance crew jump started his heart. Eight minutes. Where his spirit went somewhere else. Eight minutes.

I glance around me. We are passing Derryconnell Dump.

Were his molecules recycled? Like the paper and plastics and beer bottles there in the bottle bank. I am reminded of an old friend's epitaph: 'Returned to the Cosmos for repairs.'

People are born. People die. We must think ahead. Must look forward. Have things to look forward to. I must put aside the sadness of my Brother's anniversary. Allow excitement in.

Not many know it, but my Eldest is due to sing with the Oscar Winner. There is to be a memorial concert for my Brother, a fund raiser. One tonight in the Cork Opera House and then another in Vicar's Street in Dublin on Sunday.

What started as the seed of an idea following the funeral has become something real. Tangible. Yet again, the experts have done what experts do. With precision co-ordination by my Husband and the Archivist, there has been a collective movement of musicians, promoters, venue managers, directors that have all come together to mark my Brother's life and music. For Charity. For healing. For closure.

There is great excitement about it in the village, in the Irish music underground. On social media. Ripples of energy, bubbles of chat, snapshot smiles, pop-up conversations. In shop corridors, pavements, pub corners and Facebook, people talk about it. It is a happy energy. There is life in the village again. It is lovely to witness. I nod and share and pitch along with everybody else. Inside a sadness sits.

I don't want to burst anybody's bubble, but in spite of all the life about the place, my Brother remains dead.

Rehearsals for my Daughter are at three and so I travel to Cork. I will sneak in backstage, like the good old days, and hang stage left. It is second nature to me to seek out the stage doors. Scurry down back lanes, find discreet entrances manned by unshaved guardians in t-shirts and ripped jeans. It was learned not as a performer or stalker but from the days as a parasitic younger sister in search of her brother, or to deliver a parental message or simply ogle over a good-looking band head.

Today I pass the Opera House main entrance and skirt quay side. I bump into my Eldest. There is an excited aura to her. I am guessing on the high of pre-performance nerves. She is radiant. Aglow. She introduces me to her college colleagues. She is double jobbing it. They will film the Cork gig as part of their first year Media project. Her cohorts beam at her as she talks animatedly to me and makes introductions. She is oblivious that they are already her fans, devotees flanking their Venus.

I step into the inner sanctuary beyond the stage door and nod at the Doorman. My Eldest greets him by name. I figure she was in earlier, charmed him already. He motions silently with his head, smiling at us. We are in. My Eldest moves off with her entourage to set up cameras and do what they have to do before it is her turn to practice. I follow the curve of the cement innards as they wind up to the backstage, instinct leading me. Music floats towards me, and it is not long before I am standing in the shadow of one of the wings. I shift myself so I can look out on stage, side stepping to avoid the roadie as he scurries to and fro.

It feels familiar. Comfortable. Comforting. As if coming home, like I have been transported in time. Like it used to be at stage rehearsals in Whelan's. Bagot Street. Mother Red Caps. The old Winstanley shoe factory. 1a 2a John Dillion Street. The band room on Crane Lane. Schull. Kinsale. Our family sitting room. The band of blood-brothers, and now sisters, gathered in instrumental arms. A familiar sea of shadowed faces each bent into their own musical tool or mic. Pulsating rhythm.

Connected by music, wires, cables, and speakers. Like an ACDC vascular system threading through them all.

I recognise the voice of the Oscar Winner. He is singing my Brother's song. I find myself weeping at the nostalgic scene. Listening to an old favourite. And my Brother not here to sing it for me.

Looking for Someone

I was looking for someone,
Thought it might be you.
I was hoping for hope, my love,
Thought you'd pull me on through.

These roads keep on changing,
Broken, twisted signs on every mile.
I seriously can't remember the last time I smiled.
You are the one, my only one,
Bringing ease to my sorrow.

Well, I was looking for someone,
Thought it might be you.
I was hoping for hope, my love,
Thought you'd pull me on through.

I was frightened they'd see this man cry
In a rainy town.
I was looking at the sunlight
When the night came tumbling down.
I wandered through the darkened streets
Until I found you here.
There was brightness in your face
As you dried all of my tears.

Well I was looking for someone,
Thought it might be you.
And I was hoping for hope, my love,
Thought you'd pull me on through.

Darling take my two hands,
We will run through cracking dawn.
I seriously can't remember
What or who we're running from.
All I know is that you are the one steady thing,
You're rockin' road and worn,
Please, please stay beside me.

Well I was looking for someone,
Thought it might be you.
I was hoping for hope, my love,
Thought you'd pull me on through.

My cloud appears to shape-shift. Of late it has been reduced to slush, a slurry mixture of damp trodden wet cotton, grey from a year of filtering. Filtering and soaking. Like a cat's hair ball. A clot of mush and tears and mucous and memories. No amount of bingeing or alcohol will shift it. I have become used to how it can sludge from the cavity of my chest to lodge in the back of my throat. Sometimes it pushes up into my sinuses.

Stepping around one stage wing into another, I spy the Archivist and his wife standing looking towards the stage. How lovely, they are here too. My movement draws their eyes, and seeing me, she opens her arms. I feel the clot waiver. I step into her embrace. Tears flow. She rocks me gently, squeezing. Holding. Restoring. My cloud shape-shifts. Shedding. As if moulting. It is a soft, clean cotton ball once again.

I am wearing all black again. This time I am upping the vanity stakes. I don my Brother's *Interference* tee, having hand-altered it to fit. Boxy to Foxy. Fitted trousers, tailored jacket, high heels, hair coiffed and worn lose. A full face. Today my cheeks are sculpted, and I am wearing red on my lips. My Husband tells me I look good.

No herpes this time.

Tonight is a celebration. My Brother may be dead, but his music and memory lives on. A new album is released. *The Sweet Spot.* Our Graphics Friend produced a fervent photo-book. Souvenir T-shirts are printed.

My Brother's friends gather again in his name.

Paying it forward.

Sharing the love.

The seats fill. We take ours. Lights are up and the evening unfolds.

I am reminded of the funeral, only this is more joyous. For most.

Another favourite is sung by the Oscar Winner supported by the

Songbird. It is a trigger for my Sister-in-Law who has returned from China for the event and is sitting behind me. Her dam bursts. It is as if she has postponed grief until this moment, as if her heart is broken all over again. She sobs uncontrollably, snorts snots and gasps. I want to turn around to offer some comfort but do not so she won't lose face. I am confident that she is being quietly comforted by my Father and a Chinese cousin on either side.

On stage there is love and life.
It is bittersweet.
Time does not heal.
It just allows for longer gaps between grieving.

Something Right

I thought my problem was an empty bowl,
Until my bowl was filled.
I thought my sorrow was having to move,
Until my movement stilled.
I thought my fear was of the dark,
Until I turned on the light.
I thought that I could do nothing wrong,
Until I did something right.

I was dreaming I could touch the stars,
When I fell out of my tree.
I was always laughing at somebody else,
'til the joke turned on me.
I thought my courage meant I'd never loose,
Until I gave up the fight.
I thought that I could do nothing wrong,
Until I did something right.
Do you ever feel wonder,
but nothing to touch?

Yet touched is all you feel.
I thought of a mountain as something to climb,
And not something to rise...in me.

I thought the world was a shallow place,
'til I was lost at sea.
I thought my strength was in standing alone,
'til the ground gave beneath my feet.
And all my hopes were tied up in dreams...
Until the end of the night.

I thought that I could do nothing wrong,
Until I did something right.
I thought that I could do nothing wrong,
Until I did something right.

After the interval, a three-minute trailer for the forthcoming documentary *Breaking Out*, is played. A teaser of what could be. "A feature documentary about a man with a talent for music and life." The short clip is a slideshow of moments captured. My Brother is alive again, greeting us on the big screen. And there are snapshots of his life, with his wife, with his band, with us. There is also one with an ambulance crew. Our Documentary-Making Friend happened to be visiting during one of my Brother's close calls. The teaser is incredibly moving and funny. The story is not just about my Brother, or of music. It is a story of love. That of his for his wife and hers for him. The love between father and son.

The crowd loves it. Rapturous applause and whoops follow the call to arms, for donations. We all hunger for more. There is a vacuum in us desperate for filling. After the interval more follows. More music, more singing, more feeding.

The concert is a huge success. My Eldest performs her Irish version of "Gold" perfectly and gets a standing ovation. The Band of Brothers have adopted her. Call her their *Princess*. She is my blood, hence my Brother's blood. Kin.

A link remains.

All is good again.

Ór

Ó, 's í mo stór,
Ní mhalartóinn í ar ór.
Tá mé ag siúil ar ghéaga gealaí,
Rugadh mé le geal spúnóigín.

'S mé féin a bheidh ann,
'S bheidh mé saor ann,
Tá mé ag siúil ar ghéaga gealaí,
'S (ag) féachaint amach thar farraigí.

'S má dhúntar dhoras,
Tógtar bóthar abhaile dúinn,
'S tóg do chuirtíní síos,
Do sholas atá mar ór.

'S caithfhidh gur tú tú,
'S dein mar a dheineann tú,
Táim ag siúl ar ghéaga gealaí,
'S (ag) féachaint amach thar farraigí.

Is dá mba cré (í) do chneas,
(Cad í) an fhad a mheas tú é go mbeifeá ag tochailt?
'S da m'ba ór í do shaol,
' an fhad a mheas tú é go mbeifeá ag streachailt?

Gold

And I love her so
I wouldn't trade her for gold
I'm walking on moonbeams
I was born with a silver spoon.

Hell, I'm gonna be me
I'm gonna be free.
I'm walking on moonbeams
And staring out to sea.

And if a door be closed
Then a row of homes start building
And tear your curtains down
For sunlight is like gold.

Hey you better be you
And do what you can do
When you're walking on moonbeams
And staring out to sea.

'Cause if your skin was soil
How long do you think before they'd start digging?
And if your life was gold
How long do you think you'd stay living?

And I love her so
I wouldn't trade her for gold.

You see, life moves on.

The gaps between grieving get wider. I can breathe in-between. Life resumes. Plans are afoot. Life plans.

The Oscar winner is talking of taking my Brother's music on tour to Europe.

We can fulfil one of my Brother's other wishes and scatter some ashes at Namest Castle in the Czech Republic. My Sister-in-Law already has some of him in China. The only Western name among the many plaques lain within a beautiful flowering cemetery there. Her sister, understanding the anxiety of him being alone, bought a plot on either side of him: "So he will be surrounded by his Chinese family."

We will visit there too.

There is more talk of a second album release, my Brother's unfinished material to be finished. What will be the knock-on then?

The documentary will be finished.

Finished? Will it end then?

No.

This is a new beginning.

I will jump on board that happy caravan. It might lead to wonderful magical things.

It might all come to nothing.

But for now, what is this nothing but everything?

And a maybe a soft white cotton cloud.

I Owe You Nothing

Do the words owe the melody
Does the bird owe its song?
Do the waves owe the ocean,
Or the moonbeams the sun?
Does the dance owe the foot.
Or the foot owe the shoe?
Does the bullet owe the barrel,
Or the sniper that shoots?

Do the trees owe the forest
Does the sand owe the beach?
Do the mountains owe the heavens,
Or the hell underneath?
Does the sweet owe the sugar,
Or the sugar the sweet?
Does the bridge owe the river,
Or the house owe the street?

I owe you nothing
Except everything I own,
And all I see in my world.
And all that's left unknown.

Does the day owe the hour,
Does the year owe the week?
Does the map owe the pirate
Or the treasure he seeks?
Does the bottle owe the cork
Or the wine or the glass?
Does the question owe the answer,
Or the reason it's asked?

I owe you nothing
Except everything I own,

And all I have in truth
I only have on loan

Does the painting owe the canvas
Or the scene or the brush?
Does the suitor owe his honour
Or the virgin her blush?
Does the fruit owe the flower
Or the branch or the tree?
Did Rapunzel owe the tower
Or the honey the bee?

I owe you nothing
Except everything I own,
And all I have in truth
I only have on loan.
I owe you nothing.

DISCOGRAPHY

Song Title	Performer/ Composer	Released	QR
MY SILVER LINING	First Aid Kit [Klara & Johanna Söderberg]	2014	https://open.spotify.com/track/5BkNCux-zzid0gz9sx3NNbX?si=c-86c5078ac234851
DON'T GO DOWN	Interference [O'Farrell/ Hansard]	2005	https://interference2.bandcamp.com/track/dont-go-down
TI-TI	Interference [O'Farrell]	2010	https://interference2.bandcamp.com/track/ti-ti
SAIL ON	Interference [O Farrell/ MacClancy/ Seezer]	2006	https://interference2.bandcamp.com/track/sail-on

Song Title	Performer/ Composer	Released	QR
BLACK STAR	David Bowie [Bowie]	2016	https://open.spotify.com/track/0Fao855T3klV3RE-FRFHRF3?si=59aaa6b-9faa74c9e
PRAYER BEFORE A VOYAGE	Interference [O'Farrell/ MacClancy]	1995	https://interference2.bandcamp.com/track/prayer-before-a-voyage
LOOKING FOR SOMEONE	Interference [O'Farrell/ MacClancy/Levis]	1993	https://interference2.bandcamp.com/track/looking-for-someon
DARK DAYS	Interference [O'Farrell/Seezer]	2010	https://interference2.bandcamp.com/track/dark-days

Song Title	Performer/ Composer	Released	QR
SOMETHING RIGHT	Interference [O'Farrell/ MacClancy/ Seezer]	2008	https://interference2.bandcamp.com/track/something-right
I OWE YOU NOTHING	Interference [MacClancy/ O'Farrell]	2016	https://interference2.bandcamp.com/track/i-owe-you-nothing
GOLD	Sung by Roisin Little in Irish and by Glen Hansard in English. [O'Farrell]	2017	https://soundcloud.com/interference-archive/gold-oir
BREAKING OUT Watch the trailer for 'Breaking Out', the highly acclaimed and award-winning documentary about Fergus O'Farrell. Winner of the **Best Irish Documentary** award at the 2019 Galway Film Fleadh. Winner of the **George Morrison Feature Documentary Award** at the 2021 Irish Film & Television Academy Awards.			https://breakingoutfilm.com/

ACKNOWLEDGEMENTS

Considering it took the death of my Brother to write this book, I am not sure it is appropriate to be thanking him here, but for what it's worth, he had a wicked sense of humour, and so to that end, I say to him – your death was an inspiration, thank you.

For the many I know who feature in this book, and those who do not and are still talking to me, thank you for your ongoing support and friendship. How is it the saying goes? Be who you are and say what you want, because those that matter don't mind, and those that mind don't matter.

My Writing Friends – thank you; you know too well that need to escape and the absolute pleasure and pain that is writing. I salute you.

To Sweeney & O'Donovan – thank you for believing and giving me the platform to offload.

To Interference Band of Brothers and Sisters, and especially the Archivist, thank you for all things Ferg and for keeping me close. There are too many words…Bananas.

My Father, Mother, my Sister….. there is no limit to your love and support.

My Children whose ongoing neglect allows me to write.

My In-Laws and extended clan – thank you for loving me and all my quirks and failings.

And to my Husband – for all that you have sacrificed, mostly for what you have suffered and endured: the lonely hours, burnt dinners, empty fridge, dirty laundry. I am sorry (not sorry)

Finally, to my Sister-in-Law and Step-Nephew without whom my Brother's life would have been much shortened. Your love and support gifted us not just time but so much more. Thank you.